I AM A MAN

BLACK MEN CARE, SO TALK BACK!

DR. MICHAEL W. COUCH

Micah 6:8

4/22

CONTENTS

THE ENCOURAGEMENT WE NEED

Racism has been around for as long as we can think back, it seems. It is a subject within the halls of Congress. Many people are constantly declaring that they are not racist. However, this did not stop racism from growing. Why does racism continue when a lot of people profess to stand for equal rights for all?

Colin Kaepernick tried to bring the problems to the notice of the general public almost four years ago when he took a knee and remained that way during the National Anthem at the pro football game in which he was one of the star players. Instead of concentrating on the meaning and impact of his taking a knee, he was criticized seriously for standing against the flag of the United States of America.

During an interview, he said that he was using the position to show the public and, ultimately, the world the inequality in this country and the brutality which was often exhibited by the cops against Black and colored folks. He didn't do it for himself. He was trying to make a better world for others. Instead, he was implicated in being un-American. He eventually lost his professional position as a footballer in the NFL. But now we see the importance of what he did, where he did it. He took the opportunity to pass a message, which I believe will remain with us for as long as the U.S. will exist.

Maybe if the NFL, NBA, MLB, and others had listened four years back, all the turmoil and mayhem from George Floyd's murder might not have happened. Possibly that unfortunate death would not have happened if those issues of cops' cruelty versus Blacks had been corrected back then.

African Americans are not the only ones who are suffering from racism. Asian Americans, Latinos, Native Americans, and lots of others have suffered also. When 120,000 innocent people were removed by force from their West Coast homes and imprisoned in American concentration camps, Japanese Americans faced extreme racial hatred throughout World War II. It was mass incarceration through racial profiling, which was an outcome of racism and hatred. Yet, it is not likely that any other ethnic culture has suffered as much racism as Blacks because of the color of their skin.

Racism is bad, no matter how you view it. It should be eradicated permanently from society. It is time for people to do their part. How? By speaking against racism and injustice wherever you are and however you can. It's time to rise up. It's time to talk back.

INTRODUCTION

There is a virus that is killing the United States of America. This is worse than COVID-19 and is projected to worsen even long after the coronavirus is gone; this is racism. Racism, especially against the Black man, has increased in this 21st century.

For more than 400 years, Black folks in America have been tortured, tormented, and beaten down physically and mentally. We were even informed at one moment that we were three-fifths of an individual.

There have been numerous tranquil protests to seek justice for colored or Black people in America, such as the Selma to Montgomery March in 1965. This was a peaceful protest where all the protesters marched on a 54-mile route headed towards Alabama's state capital, where they were later met with cruelty from the cops and other outdoor groups who did not support their pursuit of equality.

Fifty-one years later, in 2016, Colin Kaepernick, a quarterback for the 49ers, took a knee throughout the National Anthem to quietly oppose the police cruelty and the injustice brought upon people of color on a day-to-day basis. Some people out there still were not getting the message. Many said that he was rude to kneel throughout the anthem.

This was a stab to the heart. Once again, people were turning a blind eye to the general message that the innocent lives of Black men, women, and children are constantly being shut down and desensitized.

"I am not going to stand up to show pride in a flag for a country that oppresses Black people and people of color," said Kaepernick to NFL Media in 2016.

There have been numerous deaths this year and fatalities last year triggered by authorities' cruelty.

Breonna Taylor, a Black woman, died on March 13, 2020. The cops were investigating two men who they supposed were selling drugs in a house that was not at all close to Taylor's home. The Louisville authorities received a "no-knock" warrant from a judge that allowed them to invade her house without recognizing themselves to look for drugs. Within a quick moment, she was shot at least eight times.

The video was released on May 8, 2020, of a Black guy named Ahmaud Arbery running in a Georgia community who died after being assaulted and shot multiple times by a father and child. The dad was a previous police officer and private investigator for the district lawyer's workplace.

On May 26, 2020, a video was launched where a white lady in New York called the police officers on a Black guy who was birdwatching in Central Park because he asked her to leash her dog. She continued to tell the cops that a Black male was threatening her and her canine.

How many deaths were triggered by authorities' brutality that was not caught on camera this year and in the past twenty years? How many officers really went to jail for murder? Unanswered questions like these make me sad and ill to the core of my stomach.

Anger, destruction, and aggravation are just a few words that describe how I feel. I am disgusted that I even have to put authorities and cruelty in the very same sentence. I'm sick of feeling stressed and anxious around the police; my parents might become another hashtag or point of observation in a Black Lives Matter movement. The idea of having my own children one day taken from me like Treyvon Martin, Eric Garner, Sandra Bland, or Philando Castile ought to not have to be a fear of mine; however, it is. This is my truth, just like lots of other Blacks and people of color in America.

We all still need to battle the oppression of Blacks in America. Nevertheless, the disturbing death of another Black guy in America, triggered by police, captured on camera, could potentially be a turning point for modification.

On May 28, 2020, video footage was launched by an officer putting his knee directly on George Floyd's neck for an estimated 8 minutes and 46 seconds. Floyd clearly stated that he couldn't breathe, but they ignored him. While Floyd was pleading for his life, the three other officers watched him being murdered right before their eyes.

After centuries of colored or Black people being lynched, incorrectly imprisoned, and eliminated by the hands of those that ought to protect us, people in America are finally opening their eyes to the horrific oppression and cruelty that is occurring within the justice system.

As Martin Luther King, Jr. famously stated, "An injustice anywhere is a threat to justice everywhere." We see it a lot lately on our TVs, individuals opposing suppressive governments that have threatened their rights, collecting in squares with signs hoping that, jointly, they can cause change. Our news media is able to capture these peoples' own armies beating them down or apprehending the leaders. We see this from the convenience of our living-room and feel completely powerless. When politics are involved, lots of private liberties are breached. Voting rights and freedom of speech are being rejected, and religious beliefs are being jeopardized while security from punishment flies out the window. When significant political systems reduce the voice of their people, others take notice.

Much more extreme than political oppressions are war criminal activities and crimes against humanity. When a nation is at war, there are constantly those individuals or groups that violate the rules of war according to global law. When individual soldiers engage in attacking non-combatants or pursuing their opponents beyond what is reasonable, they are dedicating acts of murder. In these cases, national armed forces discover themselves in a sticky situation and hardly ever stick their necks out to avoid oppression. Human rights or outdoors government activists are generally the first to take notice. Wartime conflict can also result in severe human-rights infractions, genocide, abuse, and even enslavement. These crimes breach and impact our basic rights to life, freedom, and physical security.

Those defending the rights of people worldwide will continuously see injustice occurring as long as there is a war on the planet. However, if no one protects justice, how can justice ever be done? Somebody must step up and take obligation. Human rights activists keep in mind that in order to really prevent injustice internationally, we need to aim to understand its underlying causes.

In many underdeveloped countries, there are victims of economic pressures, societal issues, and global strife. To correct some of these underlying causes of injustice, it is essential to develop programs that provide standard support for the poor, re-establish relationships between competing communities, and supply understanding and education for all victims. For those peace-building groups working to correct the wrongdoings of political oppression or wartime oppression, they have a long road ahead of them. Remember what Martin Luther King, Jr. said and take a stand whenever you can.

People all over the nation and even the world are objecting to systemic racism and police cruelty. Our voices against all the justice systems of America are not being muted anymore. Those in power are finally hearing us.

Seeing folks objecting and talking back makes me feel like there is a light at the end of the tunnel. This is definitely an indication of hope in this nation. However, there is still work to be done. Thank God for the ability of expression. The Blackman is now talking back in four ways: faith, family, fitness, and finance.

SECTION ONE

THE HISTORY OF BLACK RACISM

CHAPTER I

HOW IT ALL STARTED

IN AUGUST OF 1619, A JOURNAL ENTRY RECORDED THAT 20 or so Angolans kidnapped by the Portuguese were brought to the British colony of Virginia and were then purchased by English colonial masters.

The story of the enslaved Africans ended up being symbolic of slavery's roots. Despite captivity, Africans existed in the 1400s in America and at the dawn of 1526 in a region that would later become the United States.

Now the fate of enslaved people in the United States would divide the nation throughout the Civil War and long after the war. The racist legacy of slavery would continue, spurring movements of resistance, consisting of the Underground Railroad, the Montgomery Bus Boycott, the Selma to Montgomery March, and the Black Lives Matter movement. Through everything, Black leaders, artists, and writers have emerged to shape the character and identity of a nation.

Slavery Came to North America in 1619

To please the rapidly growing North American nests' labor requirements, white European inhabitants turned in the dawn of the 17th century from indentured servants (primarily more impoverished Europeans) to a cheaper source - oppressed Africans. After 1619, when an estranged Dutch ship brought 20 Africans ashore at the British nest of Jamestown, Virginia, slavery spread rapidly through the American nests. Though it is difficult to provide precise figures, some historians have estimated that 6 to 7 million enslaved folks were imported to the New World throughout the 18th century alone, depriving the African continent of its most important resource - its healthiest and ablest males and females.

After the American Revolution, numerous colonists (especially in the North, where slavery was reasonably unimportant to the economy) began to link the injustice of enslaved Africans to their own injustice by the British. Though leaders of then such as George Washington and Thomas Jefferson - both slaveholders and owners from Virginia - took careful steps towards restricting slavery in the newly independent country, the Constitution tacitly acknowledged the organization, guaranteeing the right to repossess anyone held to service or labor (an apparent euphemism for slavery).

Many northern states had removed slavery by the end of the 18th century; nevertheless, the organization was absolutely important to the South, where colored or Black people constituted a substantial amount of the population and the economy depended on the production of crops like tobacco and cotton. Congress prohibited the import of brand-new enslaved people in 1808; nevertheless, the enslaved population in the United States almost tripled over the next 50 years, and by 1860 it had reached practically 4 million, with over half living in the cotton-producing states of the South.

Increase Cotton Industry in 1793

In the years immediately following the Revolutionary War, the rural South - the region where slavery had taken the most significant hold in North America - dealt with an economic crisis. The soil utilized to grow tobacco, the leading money crop, was exhausted. At the same time, items such as rice and indigo stopped working to generate earnings. As a result, the rate of enslaved folks was dropping, and the ongoing growth of slavery appeared in doubt.

Around the same time, the mechanization of spinning and weaving had revolutionized England's fabric market, and the need for American cotton quickly became insatiable. Production was limited because of the tiresome procedure of removing the seeds from raw cotton fibers, which had to be finished by hand.

In 1793, a young Yankee schoolteacher named Eli Whitney created an option to solve the problem - the cotton gin. It was an easy mechanized gadget that efficiently removed the seeds. The cotton gin was extensively copied, and within a couple of years, the South would move from a dependence on the cultivation and sales of tobacco to that of cotton.

As the cotton industry's growth eventually led inexorably to an increased need for enslaved Africans, the prospect of servant rebellion, such as the one that triumphed in Haiti in 1791, drove slaveholders to make increased efforts to avoid a comparable occasion from repeating itself in the South. Likewise, in 1793, Congress passed the Fugitive Slave Act, which made it a federal criminal offense to help a shackled person attempting to leave. It was difficult to implement from state to state, specifically with the development of abolitionists in the North; the law helped legitimize and preserve slavery as a long-lasting American organization.

John Brown's Raid, October 16, 1859

A native of Connecticut, John Brown had a hard time supporting his big household. He moved uncomfortably from one state to another throughout his life, ending up being an enthusiastic opponent of slavery along with the method. After helping in the Underground Railroad out of Missouri and taking part in the bloody battle between pro - and anti-slavery forces in Kansas in the 1850s, Brown grew worried about striking a more severe blow for the cause.

On the night of October 16, 1859, John Brown led a little band of fewer than 50 men in a raid against the federal toolbox at Harper's Ferry, Virginia. They aimed to get enough ammo to lead a big operation against Virginia's slaveholders. Brown's men, including some other Black folks, captured and held the arsenal until federal and state governments sent troops and were able to subdue them.

John Brown was brought to trial on December 2, 1859. His trial riveted the country, and he became a powerful voice against all the injustice of slavery and a martyr to the abolitionist cause. As Brown's courage turned thousands of previously indifferent northerners against slavery, his violent actions convinced servant owners in the South beyond doubt that abolitionists would go to any lengths to damage the "strange organization." Rumors spread of other prepared insurrections, and the South went back to a semi-war status. After the election of the well-known anti-slavery Republican Abraham Lincoln as president in 1860, southern states began severing ties with the Union, triggering the bloodiest conflict in American history.

Civil War and Emancipation, 1861

In the spring of 1861, the bitter sectional disputes that had been increasing between the North and South throughout four years developed into the Civil War, with 11 southern states withdrawing from the Union and forming the Confederate States of America. President Abraham Lincoln's anti-slavery views were well-developed. His election as the country's very first Republican president had been the catalyst that pushed the very first southern states to withdraw in late 1860 at the start of the Civil War to abolish slavery. Lincoln sought foremost and very first to maintain the Union. He knew that a couple of people even in the North - not to mention the border slave states still loyal to Washington - would have buttressed a war against slavery in 1861.

By the fall of 1862, Lincoln believed he might not avoid the slavery concern a lot longer. Five days after the bloody Union victory at Antietam in September, he offered an initial emancipation declaration. On January 1, 1863, he made it paramount that enslaved folks within any State, or designated part of a State in disobedience, "will be then, thenceforward, and completely complimentary." Lincoln justified his decision as a wartime procedure, and as such, he did not presume relating to complimentary enslaved people in the border states committed to the Union, an omission that outraged lots of abolitionists.

By releasing an estimation of 3 million enslaved people in the rebel states, the Emancipation Proclamation denied the Confederacy of the bulk of its manpower. About 186,000 Black soldiers would later join the Union Army when the war ended in 1865, and an estimated 38,000 lost their lives. The amount of dead at war's end was 620,000 (out of a population of some 35 million), making it the costliest dispute in American history.

The Post-Slavery South of 1865

The Union's success in the Civil War gave about 4 million enslaved folks their freedom; significant challenges loomed during the Reconstruction period. The 13th Amendment, adopted late in 1865, formally eliminated slavery; however, the concern of released Black folks' status in the post-war South stayed. As white southerners gradually brought back civil authority in the previous Confederate states in 1865 and 1866, they enacted a series of laws called the Black Codes, which were developed to limit released colored or Black people's activity and ensure their accessibility as a labor force.

Along with the leniency towards the previous Confederate states by Andrew Johnson, who ended up being president after Lincoln's assassination in April 1865, so-called Radical Republicans in Congress bypassed Johnson's veto power and approved the Reconstruction Act of 1867, which basically put the South under martial law. The 14th Amendment widened the definition of citizenship, granting "equivalent security" of the Constitution to people who had been shackled. Congress needed southern states to validate the 14th Amendment and enact universal male suffrage before they might eventually rejoin the Union, and the state constitutions throughout those years were the most progressive in the region's history.

The 15th Amendment, adopted in 1870, ensured that a resident's right to vote would not be denied on account of race, color, or previous condition of the agreement. Throughout Reconstruction, Black Americans won elections to southern state governments and even to the United States Congress. Their growing influence signifi-cantly dismayed many white southerners, who felt that the control was slipping ever further far from them. The white protective soci-eties that arose throughout this duration - the largest of which was the Ku Klux Klan (KKK) - looked to disenfranchise Black people by utilizing voter suppression and intimidation in addition to more severe violence. By 1877, when the last of the federal soldiers left the South and Reconstruction subsided, Black Americans had in fact seen dishearteningly little enhancement in their financial and social status, and the political gains they had made had been cleaned away by the vigorous efforts of white supremacist forces throughout the years.

Separate but Equal, 1896

As Reconstruction waned and white supremacy forces regained control from carpetbaggers (northerners who moved South) and released Black folks, southern state legislatures started enacting the first partition laws, known as the "Jim Crow" laws. Drawn from a white actor who performed typically in Blackface, the name "Jim Crow" indicated a derogatory term for African Americans in the post-Reconstruction South. By 1885, many southern states had laws needing separate schools for White and Black trainees, and by 1900, "coloreds" were required to be separated from white people in rail-road cars and depots, hotels, theatres, dining establishments, barber stores, and other businesses. The United States Supreme Court, on May 18, 1896, provided its verdict in Plessy v. Ferguson. This case represented the first significant test of the meaning of the 14th Amendment's arrangement of full and equivalent citizenship to African Americans.

By an 8-1 bulk, the Court maintained a Louisiana law that needed the partition of passengers on railway cars and trucks. By asserting that the equal right provision was not breached as long as reasonably equivalent conditions were provided to both groups, the Court devel-oped the "different however equivalent" teaching that would there-after be utilized for assessing the constitutionality of racial partition laws. Plessy vs. Ferguson stood as the bypassing judicial precedent in civil liberties cases up until 1954 when the Court's verdict later reversed it in Brown v. Board of Education in the United States.

Washington, Carver, and Du Bois, 1900

As the 19th century came to an end and partition took a more powerful hold in the South, many African Americans saw self-improvement, specifically through education, as the single greatest chance to get away from the indignities they suffered. Various Black people looked to Booker T. Washington, the author of the bestseller *Up from Slavery* (1900), as motivation. Washington, president of Alabama's Tuskegee Normal, advised Black Americans to obtain professional or commercial training (such as farming, mechanics, and domestic service) that would offer the required abilities to make a particular niche own in the United States' economy. George Washington Carver, another formerly enslaved male and the head of Tuskegee's agriculture department, helped liberate the South from its dependence on cotton by persuading farmers to plant peanuts, soybeans, and sweet potatoes to invigorate the depleted soil.

By 1940, peanuts had turned out to be the second money crop in the South. Like Washington, Carver only had little interest in racial politics but was honored by many white or non-colored Americans as a shining example of a modest, industrious Black male. While Washington and Carver represented a technique of standing up to white supremacy, another popular Black instructor, the Harvard-trained sociologist and historian, W.E.B. Du Bois became a popular voice in the growing Black demonstration movement throughout the first half of the 20th century. Du Bois spoke highly against Washington's advocacy of commercial education in his 1903 book *The Souls of Black Folk,* which he deemed too narrow and economically focused, frustrated the value of college for African Americans.

Marcus Garvey and the UNIA in 1916

Marcus Garvey, a Black nationalist leader, was born in Jamaica, where he founded his Universal Negro Improvement Association

(UNIA) in 1914. In 1916, he brought it to the United States. Garvey, interested in the racial pride of African Americans, exalted Blackness as stunning and strong. As racial predisposition was so ingrained in white civilization, Garvey declared that it was useless for Black folks to interest white folks' sense of justice and democratic concepts. As said by him, their only hope was to run away from America and return to Africa to develop their own nation. After an unsuccessful interest in the League of Nations to settle a nest in Africa, Garvey announced the formation of the Empire of Africa in 1921, with himself as provisional president.

Other African American leaders, significantly W.E.B. Du Bois of the NAACP, slammed Garvey and his "Back to Africa" movement; he was contemptuous of them in return. There was no refuting the movement's appeal, however. Garvey, who took pride in 6 million fans in 1923, was most likely exaggerated. Still, even his criticizers admitted that the UNIA had some 500,000 members. In 1923, the United States federal government successfully found guilty and prosecuted Garvey for mail fraud in connection with offering stock in his Black Star Line shipping company. After doing a two-year jail sentence, Garvey was pardoned by President Calvin Coolidge and immediately deported. He died in London in 1940.

Harlem Renaissance in 1920

In the 1920s, the migration of Black Americans from the rural South to the metropolitan North triggered an African American cultural renaissance that took its name from the New York City neighborhood of Harlem but ended up being an extensive movement in cities throughout the North and West. Likewise referred to as the Black Renaissance or the New Negro Movement, the Harlem Renaissance marked the first time that mainstream publishers and other prominent critics seriously turned their attention to Black American literature, art, music, and politics. Blues singer Bessie Smith, bandleader Louis Armstrong, pianist Jelly Roll Morton, music composer Duke Ellington, dancer Josephine Baker, and star Paul Robeson were among the leading home entertainment artists of the Harlem Renaissance, while Paul Laurence Dunbar, Claude McKay, Langston Hughes, James Weldon Johnson, and Zora Neale Hurston were a few of its most significant authors.

There was a flip side to this higher exposure, however. Emerging Black authors relied extensively on white-owned publications houses, while in Harlem's most famous cabaret, the Cotton Club, the preeminent Black performers of the day played exclusively to white-only audiences. In 1926, a questionable bestseller about life in Harlem by the white novelist Carl von Vechten exhibited the attitude of numerous white city sophisticates, who looked to Black culture as a window into a more "primitive" and "vital" method of life. W.E.B. Du Bois, for one, railed against Van Vechten's unique and criticized works by Black writers, like McKay's novel *Home to Harlem*, that he viewed as strengthening unfavorable stereotypes of Black folks. With the start of the Great Depression, as organizations like the NAACP and the National Urban League changed their focus to the financial and political issues of Black Americans, the Harlem Renaissance waned. Its influence had stretched around the world, unlocking mainstream culture to Black artists and writers alike.

NAACP Founded in 1909

In June 1905, a group led by the famous Black educator W.E.B. Du Bois gathered at Niagara Falls, Canada, sparking a brand-new political protest movement to require civil liberties for Black people in the old spirit of abolitionism. As America's growing metropolitan population faced shortages of work and real estate, violent hostility towards Black folks had increased around the country. Lynching, though unlawful, was a prevalent practice. A wave of race riots - especially one in Springfield, Illinois in 1908 - provided a sense of seriousness to the Niagara Movement and its supporters, who in 1909 joined their agenda with that of a new permanent civil liberties organization, the National Association for the Advancement of Colored People (NAACP). Amongst the NAACP's stated goals were abolishing all forced segregation, the enforcement of the 14th and 15th Amendments, equivalent education for Black and white trainees, and total enfranchisement of all Black males. (Though supporters of female suffrage belonged to the initial NAACP, the concern was not discussed.)

Developed in Chicago, the NAACP expanded to more than 400 places by 1921. Among its earliest programs was a crusade against lynching and other lawless acts. Those efforts - consisting of a nation-wide demonstration of D.W. Griffiths' quiet movie Birth of a Nation (1915), which glorified white supremacy and the Ku Klux Klan - would continue into the 1920s, playing an important role in dramatically reducing the variety of lynchings performed in the United States. Du Bois modified the NAACP's official publication, *The Crisis,* from 1910 to 1934, releasing a number of the important voices in African American literature and politics and helping sustain the spread of the Harlem Renaissance during the 1920s.

Emmett Till, August 1955

In August 1955, a 14-year-old Black boy from Chicago named Emmett Till had recently shown up in Money, Mississippi, to visit relatives. While in a grocery shop, he allegedly whistled and made a flirtatious remark to the white lady behind the counter, breaking the stringent racial codes of the Jim Crow South. Three days later, two white males - the lady's other half, Roy Bryant, and his half-brother, J.W. Milam-- dragged Till from his uncle's home in the middle of the night.

After beating the young boy, they shot him to death and threw his body in the Tallahatchie River. The two males admitted to kidnapping Till. However, they were acquitted of murder charges by an all-white, all-male jury after hardly an hour of deliberations. Never taken to court, Bryant and Milam later shared vivid information of how they killed Till with a reporter for *Look* magazine, which released their confessions under the headline "The Shocking Story of Approved Killing in Mississippi."

Till's mother held an open-casket funeral service for her son in Chicago, wishing to bring the spotlight to the brutal murder. Thousands of mourners participated, and *Jet* magazine published an image of the corpse. International outrage over the decision and the criminal activity helped fuel the civil liberties movement. Just three months after Emmett Till's body was found, and a month after a Mississippi grand jury declined to indict Milam and Bryant on kidnapping charges, a citywide bus boycott in Montgomery, Alabama, would begin the movement with great passion.

Rosa Parks and the Montgomery Bus Boycott of December 1955

On December 1, 1955, an African American lady named Rosa Parks was riding a city bus in Montgomery, Alabama, when the chauffeur told her to relinquish her seat to a white man. Parks declined and was detained for violating the city's racial segregation ordinances, which mandated that Black guests be in the back of public buses and give their seats to white riders if the front seats were completely occupied. Parks, a 42-year-old seamstress, was also the secretary of the Montgomery chapter of the NAACP. As she later described: "I had actually been pushed as far as I could stand to be pressed. I had decided that I would need to understand at last what rights I had as a person and a resident."

Four days after Parks' arrest, an activist company called the Montgomery Improvement Association - led by a young pastor named Martin Luther King, Jr. - spearheaded a boycott of the city's municipal bus business. Since African Americans made up some 70 percent of the bus business's riders at the time, and the great bulk of Montgomery's Black people supported the bus boycott, its effect was instant.

About 90 folks in the Montgomery Bus Boycott, consisting of King, were prosecuted under a law prohibiting conspiracy to obstruct the operation of a service. Found guilty, King immediately appealed the verdict. On the other hand, the boycott stretched on for more than a year, and the bus company struggled to prevent bankruptcy.

In November 1956, in Browder v. Gayle, the United States Supreme Court promoted a lower court's decision stating that the bus business's partition seating policy was unconstitutional under the equivalent defense stipulation of the 14th Amendment. King called off the boycott on December 20, and Rosa Parks-- referred to as the "Mom of the Civil Liberties Movement" - would be one of the very first to ride the freshly integrated buses.

Central High School integrated, September 1957

The Supreme Court stated segregation of public schools illegal in Brown v. Board of Education (1954); the decision was incredibly hard to impose, as 11 southern states enacted resolutions interfering with, objecting, or nullifying school desegregation. Governor Orval Faubus in Arkansas made resistance to desegregation a central part of his effective 1956 reelection campaign.

The following September, after the desegregation of Central High School, situated in the state capital of Little Rock, Faubus spoke out to the Arkansas National Guard to prevent nine African American students from going into the school. He was later on forced to cancel the guard. In the tense standoff that followed, TV cameras recorded white mobs converging on the "Little Rock Nine" outside the high school. For countless viewers throughout the country, the memorable images provided a brilliant contrast between the mad forces of white supremacy and the quiet, dignified resistance of the African American trainees.

After an appeal by the regional mayor and congressman of Little Rock to cease the violence, President Dwight D. Eisenhower federalized the entire state's National Guard and sent out 1,000 members of the United States Army's 101st Airborne department to impose the integration of Central High School. The nine Black students got inside the school for the first time because federal soldiers had provided security for Black Americans against racial violence.

Not done combating, Faubus closed all of Little Rock's high schools in the fall of 1958 rather than permit combination. A federal court held down this act, and four of the nine students returned, under authorities' defense, in 1959 after the schools resumed.

Sit-in Movement and Founding of SNCC, 1960

On February 1, 1960, four Black students from the Agricultural and Technical College in Greensboro, North Carolina, sat at the lunch counter in a local branch of Woolworth's and purchased coffee. Refused service due to the counter's policy rule "whites-only," they stayed put until the shop closed and then returned the next day with other students. Greatly covered by the news media, the Greensboro sit-ins triggered a movement that spread rapidly throughout college towns in the South and the North. Young Black and white people participated in different types of peaceful demonstrations versus partition in libraries, beaches, hotels, and other facilities. Though many protesters were apprehended for trespassing, disorderly conduct, or interrupting the peace, their actions made an immediate impact, requiring Woolworth - amongst other facilities - to alter their segregation policies.

To take advantage of the sit-in movement's increasing momentum, the Student Nonviolent Coordinating Committee (SNCC) was established in Raleigh, North Carolina, in April 1960. Over the next couple of years, SNCC widened its impact, arranging so-called "Freedom Rides" through the South in 1961 and also the historic March on Washington in 1963; it likewise signed up with the NAACP in pressing for the passage of the Civil Rights Act of 1964. Later, SNCC would mount an arranged resistance to the Vietnam War. As its members dealt with increased violence, SNCC ended up being more militant, and by the late 1960s, it was already advocating the "Black Power" viewpoint of Stokely Carmichael (SNCC's chairman from 1966 - 67) and his follower, H. Rap Brown. By the early 1970s, SNCC was successfully disbanded.

CORE and Freedom Rides in May 1961

Established in 1942 by the civil liberties leader James Farmer, the Congress of Racial Equality (CORE) looked to end discrimination and boost race relations through direct action. In its initial years, CORE staged a sit-in at a Chicago coffeehouse (a precursor to the effective sit-in movement of 1960) and organized a "Journey of Reconciliation," in which a group of white and Black activists rode together on a bus through the upper South in 1947, a year after the United States Supreme Court forbade partition in interstate bus travel.

In Boynton v. Virginia (1960), the Court increased the length of the earlier ruling to include bus terminals, toilets, and other associated centers, and CORE took action to check the enforcement of that judgment. In May 1961, CORE sent seven African Americans and six white Americans on a "liberty ride" on two buses from Washington, D.C., bound for New Orleans. Upset segregationists attacked the liberty riders beyond Anniston, Alabama, and one bus was even firebombed. Regional police reacted, but United States Attorney General Robert F. Kennedy eventually brought State Highway Patrol security for the flexibility riders to continue to Montgomery, Alabama, where they once again encountered violent resistance.

Kennedy sent his federal marshals to escort the riders to Jackson, Mississippi, but photos of the bloodshed made the world news, and the liberty fights continued. In September, under pressure from other civil liberties companies and the CORE in addition to the chief law officer's workplace, the Interstate Commerce Commission ruled that all travelers on interstate bus providers ought to be seated without regard to race, and carriers could not mandate segregated terminals.

Integration of Ole Miss, September 1962

By the end of the 1950s, Black Americans were being accepted by only a ridiculously small number of white institutions of higher learning in the South without excessive incidents. In 1962, however, a crisis emerged when the state-funded University of Mississippi (called "Ole Miss") admitted a Black person, James Meredith. After nine years in the Air Force, Meredith had studied at the all-Black Jackson State College. With the assistance of the NAACP, Meredith submitted a claim declaring that the university had, in fact, discriminated against him due to his race. In September 1962, the United States Supreme Court ruled in Meredith's favor, but state authorities, including Governor Ross Barnett, promised to block his admission.

When Meredith reached Ole Miss under the defense of federal forces consisting of United States Marshals, a mob of more than 2,000 folks formed on the Oxford, Mississippi school. Two people were killed, and nearly 200 were hurt in the occurring turmoil, which ended only after President Kennedy's administration sent out some 31,000 soldiers to restore order. Meredith went on to graduate from Ole Miss in 1963, but the battle to incorporate college continued.

Later on that year, Governor George Wallace obstructed a Black trainee's registration at the University of Alabama, promising to "stand in the schoolhouse door." The federalized National Guard ultimately required Wallace to incorporate the university; he became a popular sign of the continued resistance to desegregation almost a decade after Brown vs. Board of Education.

Birmingham Church Bombed in 1963

Despite Martin Luther King, Jr.'s motivating words at the Lincoln Memorial throughout the historic March on Washington in August 1963, violence against Black people in the segregated South continued to show the strength of white resistance to the justice and racial consistency King upheld. In mid-September, white supremacists destroyed the 16th Street Baptist Church in Birmingham, Alabama, during Sunday services; four young African-American girls were killed in the surge. The church battle was the third in 11 days after the federal government had integrated Alabama's school system in the United States.

George Wallace, still the governor of Alabama, was a leading foe of desegregation. Birmingham also had one of the greatest and most violent views of the Ku Klux Klan. Birmingham ended up being a leading focus of the civil liberties movement by the spring of 1963 when the famous Martin Luther King, Jr. was arrested there while leading fans of his Southern Christian Leadership Conference (SCLC) in a nonviolent demonstration project against partition.

While in jail, King wrote a letter to local white ministers justifying his decision not to abort the demonstrations in the face of continued bloodshed at the hands of regional police officials, led by Birmingham's police commissioner, Eugene "Bull" Connor. "Letter from a Birmingham Jail" was released in the national press even as images of authorities' cruelty versus protesters in Birmingham - consisting of children being assaulted by cops' pet dogs and knocked off their feet by fire tubes - sent shock waves all over the world, assisting in building vital support for the civil liberties movement.

The "I Have a Dream" Speech in 1963

On August 28, 1963, some 250,000 people - both white and Black - participated in the March on Washington for Jobs and Freedom, the biggest demonstration in the history of the country's capital and the most considerable display of the civil liberties movement's growing strength. Just after marching from the Washington Monument, the demonstrators congregated near the Lincoln Memorial, where a range of civil liberties leaders dealt with the crowd needing tally rights, equal task opportunities for Black Americans, and an end to racial partition.

The last leader to come up was Martin Luther King, Jr. of the SCLC, who spoke eloquently about the plight of Black Americans and the requirement for ongoing action and nonviolent resistance. "I have a dream," King intoned, expressing his faith that one day Black and white folks would stand together and there would be consistency in between the races. "I have a dream that my four kids will one day live in a country where they will not be assessed by the color of their skin, but by the content of their character."

Martin Luther King, Jr.'s improvised sermon continued for nine minutes after completion of his prepared remarks, and his stirring words would be kept in mind as unquestionably one of the best speeches in American history. At its conclusion, King said, "Free at last! Free at last! Thank God Almighty, we are free at last!" King's speech worked as a specifying moment for the then Civil Rights Movement, and he quickly became its most prominent figure.

Civil Liberty Act of 1964 in July 1964

Thanks to the project of nonviolent resistance promoted by Martin Luther King, Jr. beginning in the late 1950s, the civil liberties movement started to gain serious momentum in the United States by 1960. That year, John F. Kennedy took the time to pass the new civil liberties legislation as part of his governmental project platform; he won more than 70 percent of the African American vote. Congress was debating Kennedy's civil liberties reform expense when he was killed by an assassin's bullet in Dallas, Texas, in November of 1963. It was now left for Lyndon Johnson (not previously known for his assistance of civil liberties) to press the Civil Rights Act - the most significant act of legislation supporting racial equality in American history - through Congress in June 1964.

At its many fundamental levels, the act gave the federal government more power to protect citizens against discrimination based on race, religious beliefs, sex, or nationwide origin. It mandated the desegregation of many public lodgings, consisting of lunch counters, bus depots, parks, and pools, and established the Equal Employment Opportunity Commission (EEOC) to ensure equal treatment of minorities in the workplace. Likewise, the act guaranteed equivalent voting rights by removing prejudiced registration requirements and procedures and licensed the United States Office of Education to supply help to school desegregation. In a telecasted ceremony on July 2, 1964, Johnson signed the Civil Rights Act into law using 75 pens; he presented one of them to King, who counted it amongst his most treasured ownerships.

Flexibility Summer and the 'Mississippi Burning' Murders in June 1964

In the summer of 1964, civil rights companies, including the Congress of Racial Equality (CORE), advised white students from the North to take a trip to Mississippi, where they assisted in signing up Black voters and building schools for Black kids. The companies thought the involvement of white students in the so-called "Freedom Summer" would bring an increased presence to their efforts.

The summer season had barely started. Nevertheless, three volunteers - Michael Schwerner and Andrew Goodman, both known white New Yorkers, and James Chaney, a Black Mississippian - disappeared on their journey back from examining the burning of an African American church by the Ku Klux Klan. After an enormous FBI investigation (code-named "Mississippi Burning"), their bodies were found on August 4, buried in an earthen dam close to Philadelphia, in Neshoba County, Mississippi.

The culprits in the case - white supremacists who consisted of the county's deputy sheriff - were quickly determined, but the state made no arrests. The Justice Department eventually indicted 19 males for breaking the three volunteers' civil liberties (the only charge that would provide the federal government jurisdiction over the case), and after a three-year-long legal fight, the men finally went on trial in Jackson, Mississippi. In October 1967, an all-white jury found seven of the offenders guilty and acquitted the other nine. Though the decision was hailed as a significant civil rights triumph (it was the very first time anybody in Mississippi had been found guilty for criminal activity of civil rights employees), the judge gave reasonably light sentences, and none of the guilty parties served more than six years behind bars.

Selma to Montgomery March in March 1965

During the early part of 1965, Martin Luther King, Jr.'s Southern Christian Leadership Conference made Selma, Alabama, the focus of its efforts to sign-up Black voters in the South. Alabama's governor, George Wallace, was an infamous opponent of desegregation, and the regional county sheriff had led a steadfast opposition to Black citizen registration drives. Only two percent of Selma's eligible Black voters had managed to register.

In February 1965, an Alabama state cannon fodder shot a young African American demonstrator in close-by Marion, and the SCLC revealed a huge protest march from Selma straight to the state capital in Montgomery years later. On March 7, 600 protesters marched as far as the Edmund Pettus Bridge outside Selma when they were assaulted by state troopers wielding whips, nightsticks, and tear gas. The brutal scene was captured on television, infuriating numerous Americans and drawing civil liberties and spiritual leaders of all faiths to join in the protest.

Martin Luther King, Jr. himself led another effort on March 9. However, he turned the marchers around when state cannon fodders once again obstructed the road. That night, a set of segregationists fatally beat up and injured a protester, the young white minister, James Reeb.

On March 21, after a United States district court coerced Alabama to allow the Selma to Montgomery March, some 2,000 marchers went on the three-day journey, this time secured by United States Army soldiers and Alabama National Guard forces under federal control. "No tide of bigotry can stop us," King declared from the actions of the state capital structure, dealing with the nearly 50,000 fans - white and Black-- who met the marchers in Montgomery.

Malcolm X Shot to Death in February 1965

In 1952, the former Malcolm Little was released from prison after serving six years on a robbery charge; while put behind bars, he had signed up with the Nation of Islam (NOI, commonly referred to as the Black Muslims), quit drinking and drugs, and changed his surname to an X to represent his rejection of his "slave" name. Eloquent and charismatic, Malcolm soon became a prominent leader of the NOI, which integrated Islam with Black nationalism and sought to motivate disadvantaged young Black people looking for confidence in the segregated United States of America.

As the outspoken and organized public voice of the Black Muslim faith, Malcolm challenged the mainstream civil liberties movement and the nonviolent pursuit of combination championed by Martin Luther King, Jr. Instead, he advised fans to safeguard themselves against white hostility "by any means necessary." Mounting stress between Malcolm and NOI founder Elijah Muhammad led Malcolm to form his own mosque in 1964. He made a trip to Mecca that same year and underwent a second conversion to Sunni Islam. Calling himself El-Hajj Malik El-Shabazz, he renounced NOI's separatism approach and promoted a more inclusive method to the struggle for all Black rights.

On February 21, 1965, three NOI members shot Malcolm 15 times in close proximity during a speaking engagement in Harlem. After Malcolm's death, his successful book, *The Autobiography of Malcolm X*, promoted his ideas, specifically amongst Black youth, and set the foundation for the Black Power movement of the late 1960s and 1970s.

Ballot Rights Act in August 1965

Just less than a week after the Selma-to-Montgomery marchers were beaten and bloodied by Alabama state cannon fodders in March 1965, President Lyndon Johnson addressed Congress's joint session, requiring federal legislation to ensure the security of the ballot rights of African Americans. The outcome was the Voting Rights Act, which Congress passed in August 1965.

The Voting Rights Act looked to eliminate the legal barriers that still existed at the state and regional level preventing Black residents from exercising the right to vote offered them by the 15th Amendment. Particularly, it banned literacy tests as a requirement for voting, mandated federal oversight of citizen registration in locations where tests had formerly been used, and offered the United States Attorney General the responsibility of challenging making use of poll taxes for state and regional election.

In combination with the Civil Rights Act of the preceding year, the Voting Rights Act was among the most extensive pieces of civil liberties legislation in American history, and it considerably lowered the variation between white and Black citizens in the United States. In Mississippi alone, the portion of qualified Black voters signed up to vote increased from 5 percent in 1960 to almost 60% in 1968. In the mid-1960s, 70 Black Americans worked as elected officials in the South, while by the end of the century, there were close to 5,000. In the same period, the variety of Blacks serving in Congress increased from six to almost forty.

CHAPTER II

RISE OF BLACK POWER

AFTER THE POTENT RUSH OF THE CIVIL RIGHTS Movement's first years, anger and aggravation increased among many African Americans, who saw plainly that real equality - social, political, and financial - still eluded them. In the late 1960s and early 1970s, this disappointment sustained the rise of the Black Power movement. According to then SNCC chairman, Stokely Carmichael, who first promoted the term "Black Power" in 1966, the conventional Civil Rights Movement and its focus on nonviolence did not go far enough, and the federal legislation it had achieved stopped working to attend to the economic and social disadvantages dealing with Black Americans.

Black Power was a type of both self-definition and self-defense for African Americans; it forced them to stop seeking the institutions of white America - which were thought to be inherently racist - and act by themselves to seize the gains they preferred, such as better jobs, real estate, and education. In 1966, Huey P. Newton and Bobby Seale, college trainees in Oakland, California, established the Black Panther Party.

While its original objective was to secure Black folks from white cruelty by sending out patrol groups into Black communities, the Panthers quickly developed into a Marxist group that promoted Black

Power by advising African Americans to arm themselves and demand full work, good real estate, and control over their own people. Clashes arose between the Panthers and police in New York, California, and Chicago, and in 1967 Newton was found guilty of voluntary manslaughter after eliminating a law enforcement officer. His trial brought national attention to the party, which at its peak in the late 1960s boasted some 2,000 members.

Fair Housing Act in April 1968

The Fair Housing Act of 1968, regarded as a follow-up to the Civil Rights Act of 1964, marked the last excellent legislative achievement of the civil liberties period. Initially intended to extend federal security to civil rights employees, it was later broadened to resolve racial discrimination in the sale, rental, or funding of real estate systems. After the expense passed the Senate by an extremely narrow margin in early April, it was believed that the increasingly conservative House of Representatives, wary of the growing strength and militancy of the Black Power movement, would weaken it significantly.

On the day of the Senate vote, however, Martin Luther King, Jr. was assassinated in Memphis. The pressure to pass the expense increased amidst the wave of national remorse that followed, and after a strictly minimal debate, the House passed the Fair Housing Act on April 10. President Johnson signed it into law the subsequent day. Over the next years, there was little decrease in real estate segregation, and violence developed from Black efforts to look for housing in white communities.

From 1950 up until 1980, the overall colored population in America's city centers rose from 6.1 million to 15.3 million; throughout this same period, white Americans progressively moved out of the cities into the suburban areas, taking with them a lot of the job opportunities Black folks needed. In this way, the "ghetto" - an inner-city community afflicted by high joblessness, criminal activity, and other social ills - ended up being an ever more common fact of metropolitan Black life.

MLK Assassinated on April 4, 1968

On April 4, 1968, the world was saddened and stunned by the news that the civil liberties activist and Nobel Peace Prize winner Martin Luther King, Jr. had been shot and eliminated on the terrace of a motel in Memphis at the place where he had gone to support a sanitation workers' strike. King's death opened a big rift between white and Black Americans, as numerous Black people saw the killing as a denial of their energetic pursuit of equality through the nonviolent resistance he had promoted. Several days of riots, burning, and looting followed his death in more than a hundred cities.

The accused killer, a white man named James Earl Ray, was apprehended and arrested instantly; he went into a guilty plea and was sentenced to 99 years in jail; no testament was heard. Ray later recanted his confession, and despite several inquiries into the matter by the United States government, many continued to believe that the speedy trial had been a cover-up for a much larger conspiracy. Martin Luther King, Jr's assassination, along with the killing of Malcolm X three years prior, radicalized lots of moderate African American activists, fueling the growth and increase of the Black Power movement and the Black Panther Party.

The success of conservative political leaders that year - including Richard Nixon's election as president of the country and the third-party candidacy of the ardent segregationist George Wallace, who won 13 percent of the vote - dissuaded African Americans, a lot of whom felt that the tide was turning against the Civil Rights Movement.

Shirley Chisholm Runs for President in 1972

In the early 1970s, the advances of the Civil Rights Movement had integrated with the increase of the feminist movement to develop an African American female's movement. "There can't be liberation for only half of a race," declared Margaret Sloan, one of the women behind the National Black Feminist Organization, established in 1973. A year prior, Representative Shirley Chisholm of New York became a national symbol of both movements as the first significant party African American candidate and the first female prospect for United States president.

A previous instructional expert and a founder of the National Women's Caucus, Chisholm became the first Black woman in Congress in 1968 when she was chosen to the House from her Brooklyn district. Although she failed to win a primary, Chisholm got more than 150 votes at the Democratic National Convention. She claimed she never anticipated winning the nomination. It later went to George McGovern, who then lost to Richard Nixon in the general election.

The outspoken Chisholm, who brought in little support amongst African American males during her governmental project, later informed journalists: "I've constantly satisfied more discrimination being a lady than being Black. When I contested for the Congress, when I contested for president, I fulfilled more discrimination as a female than for being Black."

The Bakke Decision and Affirmative Action in 1978

Starting from the 1960s, the term "affirmative action" was utilized to refer to initiatives and policies focused on making up for previous discrimination on the basis of race, color, sex, religion, or national origin. President John F. Kennedy initially used the expression in 1961 to call on the federal government to hire more African Americans. By the mid-1970s, many universities were looking to increase minority and female professors and students on their campuses. The University of California (UCLA) at Davis, for instance, designated 16 percent of its medical school's admissions spots for minority candidates.

After Allan Bakke, a white California man, applied two times without success, he sued U.C. Davis, declaring that his grades and test ratings were higher than those of minority trainees who were accepted and accusing UC Davis of "reverse discrimination." In June 1978, in the case of Regents of the University of California vs. Bakke, the United States Supreme Court ruled that using stringent racial quotas was unconstitutional. On the other hand, it held that colleges might rightfully utilize race as a criterion in admissions choices to ensure variety.

In the wake of the Bakke verdict, strong action continued to be a dissentious and controversial concern, with a growing opposition movement declaring that the so-called "racial playing field" was now equivalent. In this way, African Americans no longer required a unique consideration to conquer their disadvantages. In subsequent decisions over the next years, the Court limited the scope of affirmative action programs, while a number of states prohibited racially based action.

Jesse Jackson Galvanizes Black Voters in 1984

When he was young, Jesse Jackson left his studies at the Chicago Theological Seminary to sign up with the SCLC in its movement for Black civil rights in the South; when Martin Luther King, Jr. was assassinated in Memphis in April 1968, Jackson was at his side. In 1971, Jackson established PUSH, or People United to Save Humanity (later on altered to People United to Serve Humanity), an organization that promoted self-reliance for African Americans and looked to establish racial parity in business and finances.

Jackson was a leading voice for Black Americans throughout the early 1980s, advising them to be more politically active by heading up a citizen registration drive that led to the election of Harold Washington as the first Black mayor of Chicago in 1983. The following year, Jackson ran for the Democratic elect for president. On the backing of his Rainbow/PUSH Coalition, he placed third in the primaries, moved by an increase of Black voter involvement.

He ran again in 1988 and got 6.6 million votes, or 24 percent of the overall primary vote, winning seven states and finishing second behind the ultimate Democratic nominee, Michael Dukakis. In the decades that followed, Jackson's continued impact in the Democratic Party guaranteed that African American's problems had a crucial role in the celebration's platform. Throughout his long profession, Jackson has motivated both admiration and criticism for his vigorous efforts on behalf of the Black community and his outspoken personality. His son, Jesse L. Jackson, Jr., won the election to the United States House of Representatives in 1995.

Oprah Winfrey Started Syndicated Talk Show, 1986

During the 1980s and 1990s, the success of the long-running comedy The Cosby Show - featuring popular comedian Bill Cosby as the medical professional patriarch of a close-knit middle-class African American family - helped redefine the image of Black characters on traditional American television. Suddenly, there were more informed, upwardly mobile, family-oriented Black characters for television audiences to look to, both in fiction and in life.

In 1980, entrepreneur Robert L. Johnson established Black Entertainment Television (BET), which he later sold to home entertainment giant Viacom for $3 billion. Perhaps the most striking phenomenon, nevertheless, was the rise to fame of Oprah Winfrey.

Oprah Winfrey was born in rural Mississippi to a poor unwed teenage mom; Winfrey got her start in television news before taking control of an early morning talk program in Chicago in 1984. Two years later, she introduced her own nationally syndicated talk program, The Oprah Winfrey Show, which would later become the highest-rated show in television history. Praised for her capability to talk openly about a wide variety of problems, Winfrey spun her talk show success into a one-woman empire, consisting of acting, movie and tv productions, and publishing.

She especially promoted the work of Black female authors, forming a movie business to produce films based on books like *The Color Purple* by Alice Walker and *Beloved* by Nobel Prize winner Toni Morrison. (She starred in both.) One of the most prominent people in entertainment and the first Black female billionaire, Winfrey is also an active benefactor, offering kindly to Black South Africans and Morehouse College, among other causes.

Los Angeles Riots in 1992

In March 1991, California Highway Patrol officers attempted to pull over an African American man named Rodney King for speeding on a Los Angeles highway. King, who was on probation for a break-in, and had been drinking, led them on a high-speed chase. By the time patrolmen caught up to his vehicle, numerous officers of the Los Angeles Police Department were on the scene. After King supposedly resisted arrest and threatened them, four LAPD officers shot him with a TASER weapon and badly beat him.

Captured on videotape by an observer and broadcasted worldwide, the whipping inspired extensive outrage in the city's African American neighborhood, which had long condemned the racial profiling and wrongful abuse its members suffered from the police force. Many required that the out-of-favor L.A. police chief, Daryl Gates, be fired and the four officers be taken to court for their excessive force with King. The King case was ultimately tried in the suburban area of Simi Valley, and in April 1992, a small jury found the officers not guilty.

Rage over the decision sparked the four days of the L.A. riots, starting in the primarily Black South Central neighborhood. By the time the riots ended, 55 people were dead, more than 2,300 were injured, and more than 1,000 structures had been burned. Authorities later projected the total damage at around $1 billion. The next year, two of the four LAPD officers associated with the beating were retried and convicted in a federal court for breaching King's civil rights; he eventually got $3.8 million from the city in a settlement.

Million Man March, 1995

In October 1995, hundreds of countless Black males collected in Washington, D.C. for the Million Man March, one of the largest presentations of its kind in the capital's history. Its organizer, Minister Louis Farrakhan, had required "a million sober, disciplined, dedicated, inspired Black guys to meet in Washington on a day of atonement." Farrakhan, who had asserted control over the Nation of Islam (typically known as the Black Muslims) at the end of the 1970s and reasserted its initial concepts of Black separatism, may have been an incendiary figure. However, the Million Man March idea was one most Blacks (and many whites) might get behind.

The march was meant to produce a sort of spiritual renewal among Black males and impart them with a sense of solidarity and individual duty to enhance their condition. Likewise, organizers believed it would negate some of the stereotyped unfavorable images of Black males that existed in American society.

By that time, the United States government's "war on drugs" had sent a disproportionate number of African Americans to jail, and by 2000, more Black men were put behind bars than in college. Estimates of the people in the Million Man March ranged from 400,000 to more than 1 million, and its success stimulated the company of a Million Woman March, which occurred in Philadelphia in 1997.

Colin Powell Became Secretary of State in 2001

As the chairman of the Joint Chiefs of Staff from 1989 to 1993, the first African American to hold that position, the Vietnam veteran and four-star United States Army General Colin Powell played an essential role in planning and carrying out the Persian Gulf War, which happened under the term of President George Bush. Soon after he left the military in 1993, many people began floating his name as a possible presidential prospect. He chose to run, and though he did not win, he became a prominent fixture in the Republican Party.

In 2001, George W. Bush appointed Powell as Secretary of State, making him the first African American to act as America's top diplomat. Powell looked to build global assistance for the controversial U.S. invasion of Iraq in 2003, providing a dissentious speech to the United Nations relating to that nation's possession of weapons later revealed to be based upon malfunctioning intelligence. He resigned after Bush's reelection in 2004.

In another history-making visit, Condoleezza Rice, Bush's longtime diplomacy advisor and the previous head of the National Security Council, became the first African American woman to function as Secretary of State. Staying out of the political spotlight after stepping down, Powell stayed an appreciated figure in Washington and beyond.

He went on to brush off any speculation of a possible future presidential run. Throughout the 2008 governmental campaign, Powell made headlines when he broke from the Republican party to back Barack Obama, the eventual winner and first African American to be elected president of the United States.

Barack Obama Became 44th United States President in 2008

By January 20, 2009, Barack Obama was inaugurated as the 44th president of the United States; he was the first African American to hold that office. The product of interracial marriage (his dad grew up in a little town in Kenya, his mother in Kansas), Obama grew up in Hawaii. He discovered his civic calling in Chicago, where he worked for numerous years as a neighborhood organizer on the city's mostly Black south side.

After schooling at Harvard Law School and practicing constitutional law in Chicago, he began his political life in 1996 in the Illinois State Senate. In 2004, he put in a bid for his candidateship for a recently vacated seat in the United States Senate. He provided a rousing keynote speech at that year's Democratic National Convention, drawing in national attention as he eloquently spoke about national unity and cooperation throughout party lines. In February 2007, simply months after he became the third African American chosen to the United States Senate, Obama announced his candidateship for the 2008 Democratic presidential nomination.

After holding up against a tight Democratic main fight with Hillary Clinton, the former first lady and New York senator, Obama defeated Senator John McCain of Arizona in the general election that November. Obama's looks in both the primaries and the general election drew impressive crowds, and his message of hope and modification - embodied by the motto "Yes We Can" - inspired countless new citizens, many young and Black, to cast their vote for the very first time in the historic election. He was reelected in 2012.

The Black Lives Matter Movement in 2020

The term "Black Lives Matter" was initially utilized by organizer Alicia Garza in a July 2013 Facebook post in action to the acquittal of

George Zimmerman, a Florida male who shot and killed an unarmed 17-year-old, Trayvon Martin, on February 26, 2012. Martin's death triggered nationwide demonstrations like the Million Hoodie March. Patrisse Cullors, Alicia Garza, and Opal Tometi formed the Black Lives Matter Network with the objective to "eliminate white supremacy and build local power to intervene in violence inflicted on Black communities by the state and vigilantes."

The hashtag #BlackLivesMatter initially appeared on Twitter on July 13, 2013, and spread widely as prominent cases involving the unfortunate deaths of Black civilians provoked a huge outrage. Later, a series of deaths of Black Americans at the hands of white policemen continued to stimulate outrage and protests, consisting of Michael Brown in Ferguson, Missouri, Eric Garner in New York City, New York, Freddie Gray in Baltimore, Maryland, and Tamir Rice in Cleveland, Ohio.

The Black Lives Matter Movement gained commercial media attention on September 25, 2016, when San Francisco 49ers' players Eric Reid, Eli Harold, and quarterback Colin Kaepernick kneeled throughout the nationwide anthem before the game versus the Seattle Seahawks to draw attention to recent acts of police cruelty. Dozens of other football players in the NFL and beyond followed suit.

George Floyd Protests in 2020

The movement swelled to a crucial juncture on May 25, 2020, amid the dreaded COVID-19 epidemic, when 46-year-old George Floyd died after being handcuffed and pinned to the ground by policeman Derek Chauvin.

Chauvin was kneeling on Floyd's neck for more than 8 minutes. Floyd had been accused of utilizing a fake $20 bill at a local deli in Minneapolis. All four officers associated with the event were fired, and Chauvin was charged with second-degree murder, third-degree murder, and second-degree manslaughter. The three other officers were charged with assisting and abetting murder.

Floyd's murder came about on the heels of two other high-profile cases in 2020. On February 23, 25-year-old Ahmaud Arbery was killed while out on a jog after being followed by three white men in a pickup truck. And on March 13 of the same year, 26-year-old EMT Breonna Taylor was shot eight times and killed after authorities broke down the door to her home in the middle of the night.

On May 26, 2020, the day after Floyd's unfortunate murder, protestors in Minneapolis flooded the streets to object to Floyd's killing. Police automobiles were set on fire, and officers released tear gas to disperse crowds. After months of quarantine and isolation throughout the global pandemic, demonstrations started spreading throughout the nation.

SECTION TWO

OTHER RACISM

CHAPTER III

RACISM IN INSTITUTIONS

When we think about racism in schools, we are constantly drawn back to the concept of segregated bathrooms, sitting at the back of the bus, and negative comments made to students of some spiritual or ethnic minority. A larger issue in today's school is the idea of institutional racism, one that is not as quickly seen. However, the impacts are the same.

In May 1998, a teacher named Evelyn Hanssen wrote a piece entitled "A White Teacher Reflects on Institutional Racism." In this piece, she cites several occurrences of institutional racism that she felt had an extensive impact on both the students and the faculty, even though the majority of the time they may not have actually even understood it. We will be looking at these ideas regarding a chapter in Malcolm X's autobiography to show and offer examples from a famous case in American history.

Institutional Racism: Discussion Based Upon Hanssen and Malcolm X.

Most of the time, when teachers first enter the workforce, they envision having a favorable influence on their student's lives. They believe that they will be exempt from bias and labeling, which will provide every trainee with an equal opportunity at learning. This is exactly what Evelyn Hanssen wanted and speaks about in her piece on institutional racism. However, she discovered that not all things work out in reality as we would ideally have them to be.

It was amazing to her that her associates - supposedly informed people - were making racial biases. Even though they may not have understood they were doing it, the biases were still occurring. In one circumstance, she sat in on an English department meeting in order to choose the new curriculum for the trainees. She was amazed to discover that many African American's works were turned down, even though they were a much better fit for the classes, on the basis that they were too raunchy (Hanssen 1998). She was also shocked to see an obviously certified African American mentor candidate ignored for an inferior white individual for a position opening in her school.

When questioning the administrator about the hiring, she was informed that while it is crucial to work with minorities, it was tough to find suitable candidates. She was given an example of circular logic that never ever quite discussed why the African American prospect was not hired when Hanssen advised the person about the overlooked candidate. This concept is the basis for her entire paper: that individuals, although they may not understand it, do hold some racism concepts, which can extensively impact minority trainees, as shown in Malcolm X's autobiography.

In Malcolm X's autobiography, there is a chapter entitled "Mascot," where he describes his school experiences that result in him becoming what he was. In the chapter, he discusses examples of institutional racism and that he was the only Black student in his class. Many of the instances he describes, though awful, were acceptable during that time.

The overuse of the word "nigger", while certainly something that is suggested to separate Malcolm from the other students, did not appear to be as damaging. However, as he puts it, he was something of a quirk, sort of like a pink poodle, and even though he was not expected to talk with the white girls or show any sort of ethnic pride, he was seen as a mascot of sorts, something different that people somehow gravitated to based just on one aspect of his character, his skin. (Malcolm X, 1964).

Being a mascot might have looked like something that was an advantage in some respects. However, what Malcolm viewed as acceptance would be categorized as institutional racism today. He provided an example of when he attended a class taught by who he thought was an outstanding instructor since he constantly helped him along. However, when Malcolm revealed the desire to become an attorney, the teacher essentially made fun of him and told him that he needed to understand that he would never ever be a lawyer as an African American. He was told that it would be much better for him to be a carpenter.

This is extremely much a circumstance of institutional racism, for even the instructor believed that he was assisting Malcolm by telling him how he perceived the world works; in reality, he was obstructing Malcolm's ability to be who he wished to be. What occurs in these circumstances is the same thing that occurs way too frequently. As you could probably imagine, that instructor was no longer a favorite of Malcolm's after that incident, and he feared going to the man's class, believing differently now about the instructor than before the racist remarks were made.

We are all familiar with racist practices in Nazi Germany and South Africa. Now that apartheid is in the past, that is not to state that racism does not exist.

The first change in racism includes taking a look at the type of difference underpinning racism. Originally, racism was based upon biology, e.g., the Nazis wished to develop a blond, blue-eyed Aryan race. The idea was that biologically determined distinction ought to equate to the social hierarchy (International Human Rights Lexicon by Marks and Clapham). Nevertheless, distinctions between individuals are viewed as less about look and genes and more about the experiences and history that have influenced their cultural identity. Today, social variety is celebrated, but there is a paradox. Social life works best when people stick with their own kind. In the current environment, racism is likely to be more based upon culture than upon biology.

Another emerging trend is a modification in the practice of racism. Whereas formerly individuals were segregated, dominated, and eliminated (genocide) in Nazi Germany and South Africa, this is less likely to occur in the modern world (although Rwanda and Yugoslavia are not too far back in our memories). Nowadays, we must take a look at racism in the context of public and personal organizations.

In the UK, the timeless example of this is the Stephen Lawrence Enquiry. Two Black teens were assaulted and killed by a group of white youths, none of whom were charged. The inquiry report found that there had actually been a combination of professional incompetence, failure of management, and racism. The racism included could not be understood as a series of private racially determined acts. However, they had rather be considered a case of institutional racism. The Americans refer to an offense called "driving while Black." In other words, there is overwhelming evidence of instances of Black Americans being stopped while driving just because they are Black.

The third modification is in context. The primary shift is one from accepted racism within colonial societies to official anti-racism. If a business includes an expression in its objective statement announcing "equivalent opportunity for all," that does not always mean there are no racist practices in that organization. Since nobody desires to confess that it is going on, such declarations may help sustain the denial or repression of racism.

Another anomaly is that while in the contemporary world, products and services can be sent out from one end of the world to the other with relative ease, there has been a fantastic clampdown on individuals' free movement. Immigrants still tend to be seen with suspicion in their host nations, but much of these are just good, dedicated individuals attempting to provide and make a living for their households.

Racism Against Asians

African Americans have struggled with racism for a lot of years. Race and the color of one's skin must not be a factor to hate. Once again, racism has made its way to the forefront after the terrible killing of George Floyd in Minneapolis. Police cruelty and racism have been looked upon as the reason for his unfortunate death. There is much chaos, as thousands of individuals are opposing racism.

Asian Americans have likewise been the victims of racism for many years, although they are now thought about as the "design minority" by much of the population. They are considered as being passive and accepting of their fate without a problem. They are understood as quiet Americans due to their past actions of conquering some of the racism they dealt with. However, they still deal with racism, though not as routinely or as extreme as Black individuals. Additionally, some Asian Americans have recently encountered racism by being blamed for the coronavirus.

The first Asians to come to the United States were Filipino sailors who got here around 1750 in Louisiana. Asians came to the United States in larger numbers in 1848 when gold was found in California. They attempted their luck at the fortune which appeared to be offered. They had prepared to return to their houses as rich people. Other Chinese people went to Hawaii to work in different sugarcane plantations. They also worked as garden enthusiasts, domestics, laundry employees, and in farming. Some ended up being merchants. An estimated 9,000 to 12,000 Chinese dealt with the railway in the most dangerous jobs; however, they were paid less than their European counterparts.

Immigrant Chinese males were a major force in the building of the Transcontinental Railroad. These were workers who assisted with constructing the infrastructure of America. They dealt with racism and were omitted from the event held near Promontory Point in Utah when the railway came together over 150 years ago. Their crucial efforts were overlooked in the history books until more recent times.

There was a Chinese Exclusion Act versus the Chinese in 1882 to stop additional migration. Japanese immigrants then started to enter the United States in the late 1800s and early 1900s. Then in 1924, there was a notable act to prevent more immigration from ancient Japan. These were acts that encouraged racism and hate for those people who were different from the mainstream population of the United States.

When Japanese Americans and their immigrant moms and dads were forcibly removed from their west coast homes, potentially the broadest sweeping example of racism versus Asian Americans came during World War II. These individuals were innocent of any incorrect doing and lost nearly everything they owned because of racism and hatred. This was known as mass racial profiling at its worst.

There have been individual cases of severe racism against Asian Americans. An example is Vincent Chin, who was a young Chinese American. Vincent was a young male who was to be married. He and some of his friends were celebrating with a bachelor party in Detroit when Japanese import automobiles started to gain favor with Americans after an extreme gas shortage.

Vincent and his pals were confronted by two white former employees of the automobile industry. The guy and his stepson, who had been laid off from his job in an auto plant, were upset at Japan and anybody viewed as Japanese. After a preliminary conflict, the groups broke up. The white men drove around for about 20 minutes, trying to find Vincent and his pals. They found them at a McDonald's, where the conflict continued and intensified.

In the end, Vincent was dead from being beaten mercilessly with a baseball bat. The two guys pleaded guilty to the crime but were not subjected to any prison time. Asian Americans were understandably outraged.

Many Asian Americans have been called racial slurs. They have been told to return to where they came from, although they were born in the United States. They are often referred to as "continuous foreigners" merely because of their physical attributes.

Many African Americans and Asian Americans (and other ethnic groups) have succeeded despite racism in this nation. Racism is still a major issue. Asian Americans have typically not dealt with racism as frequently and as significantly as numerous African Americans continue to do so. Asian Americans and other minorities stand in uniformity with Black individuals in condemning racism and working for reform to relieve racial tensions. Everyone should have to be dealt with fairly and equitably without racism clouding the picture.

Significant Areas of Racism

Those who either proclaim or articulate a message stating there is no such thing as systemic racism in this country are either burying their heads in the sand, in denial, or part of the issue! In nearly every element of life, we witness some degree of this dreadful behavior and have done so for generations. Since the rhetoric and vitriol of President Donald Trump, some of these haters may have felt enabled and entitled. The ugly face of racism has become even more obvious and widespread!

Have we been exposed to such numerous hate crimes, White Supremacist presentations, etc.? Perhaps, the systemic racism might be more disturbing because, up until recently, there has been little attempt at a national conversation about the requirement to face the facts and attend to the concern. With that in mind, this book will attempt to briefly address five substantial areas that need to see change.

1. *Education*: Many inequities begin with the variation in the quality of education provided in our wealthiest and poorest communities. When this becomes more comparable, we will begin to be able to reduce some of the numerous future injustices. Statistics teach us that minority communities mostly get the least quality education and experience the greatest difficulties regarding drop-products, delinquencies, equipment, etc. Unless a higher degree of nationwide resources and focus is placed on viable solutions to these injustices, we will not make much progress in battling this obstacle!

2. *Quality real estate*: For a range of reasons, including financial, task security, education, etc., most public real estate has minority residents! Many of these experience security issues, criminal offense concerns, fears, weak points, weak infrastructures (interior and exterior), tidiness, and sanitation problems. Today, the dreadful pandemic must have taught us that minorities are often hardest hit, and the combination of inadequate education and quality real estate is significant to this equation.

3. *Criminal justice/policing*: Few open-minded individuals reject that minorities do not receive equal justice, rights, and liberties. Many

police departments have typically treated individuals of color differently from others! Numerous examinations of how culprits are dealt with by our criminal justice system deny there is a systemic form of racism when it comes to equal enforcement of the law and representation.

4. *Employment*: The failures, in terms of how we educate, wind up with substantial implications regarding work chances, and so on. Stats also indicate many major distinctions in job opportunities, incomes, and types. In addition, in far too numerous cases, individuals today are still discriminated against based on ethnicity and racial background.

5. *Healthcare*: Many minority groups do not get the same quality of healthcare or have access to the finest hospitalities (with the best devices, etc.).

Put yourself in the place of minority members who face additional obstacles and often overt, systemic racism in almost every area of life! Shouldn't America honor its commitment to equal justice and rights, no matter the color of one's skin?

SECTION THREE

MISCONCEPTIONS IN BLACK RACISM

CHAPTER IV

MISCONCEPTION OF THE HISTORICAL OPPRESSION OF THE BLACK MAN

WITH REALITIES CAME MISTAKEN BELIEFS, SPECIFICALLY to Black history and injustice, including the Tuskegee experiment and enslaved folks' finances.

To study American history is typically an exercise in finding out patriotic fables and partial realities. Textbooks and educational manuals worldwide continue to center the white experience with Black people frequently quarantined to a short section about slavery and quote MLK Jr. Numerous amounts leave their high school history class with a misunderstanding of the historical perspective of Black people in America.

Last summer, the New York Times's 1619 Project burst open a long-overdue discussion about how stories of Black Americans need to be informed through the lens of Black Americans themselves. In this custom, and during Black History Month, Vox asked six Black scholars and historians about myths surrounding Black history. Ultimately, understanding Black history is more than simply learning about the brutality and injustices Black folks have endured; it's about the methods they have fought to make it through and flourish in America.

Misconception: Black people in early Jim Crow America did not fight back

We all know that African Americans faced the constant danger of ceremonial public executions by white mobs, unpunished attacks by people, and police brutality in Jim Crow America. How they responded to this is a myth that persists. In an effort to find legal ways to deal with such occasions, some Black people made legalistic attempts to convince police and civic leaders that their rights and lives ought to be safeguarded. Yet, the squashing weight of a hostile criminal justice system and the rigidity of the color line typically silenced those petitions, leaving Black folks susceptible to more mistreatment and murder.

In the face of this violence, some Black Americans prepared themselves physically and mentally for the abuse they felt was in store, and they resisted. Distressed by public racial violence and reluctant to accept it, various Blacks followed emerging ideologies of outright disobedience, specifically after the turn of the 20th century and the advancement of the "New Negro."

For New Blacks, the comparatively tame efforts of groups like the NAACP were not immediate enough. They secured themselves increasingly nationwide throughout the bloodshed of the Red Summer of 1919 when whites assaulted African Americans in multiple cities throughout the country. Whites might have started most race riots in the early Jim Crow age; nevertheless, some similarly occurred as Black folks turned down the restrictions placed on their life, labor, and leisure. Furthermore, when they declined to fold under the force and pressure of white supremacy, the magnitude of racial and state violence typically bared down upon Black folks who protected themselves from cops and citizens. However, that did not stop some from sparking individual and cumulative insurrections.

Misconception: That Black innovative soldiers were patriots

Much is made about how colonial Black Americans - some totally free, some enslaved - battled during the American Revolution. Black revolutionary soldiers are generally called Black Patriots. However, the term patriot is reserved within advanced discourse to refer to the males of the 13 nests who believed in the concepts expressed in the Declaration of Independence: that America needs to be an independent country devoid of Britain. These persons were ready to combat for this cause and sign up with the Continental Army. For their sacrifice, they were permanently thought of as patriots. That's why the phrase Black Patriot is a myth - it presumes that Black and white advanced soldiers defended the very same factors.

Black revolutionary soldiers did not combat out of love for a nation that oppressed and suppressed them. Black revolutionary soldiers were combating for freedom - not for America but for themselves and the race. In reality, the American Revolution is a case study of interest convergence. Interest convergence signifies that within racial states such as the 13 nests, any development made for Black folks can only be made if that development likewise benefits the dominant culture - in this case, the freedom of the white colonists of America. To put it simply, colonists' enlistment of Black folks was not out of some ethical requirement; it was based on the workforce's needs to win the war.

In 1775, Lord Dunmore, the royal governor of Virginia who wished to rapidly end the war, provided a pronouncement to totally free enslaved Black people if they defected from the colonies and defended the British army. In response to this, George Washington revised the policy that limited Blacks (free or enslaved) from joining his Continental Army. His reversal was based on merging his interests: completing with a growing British military, securing the slave economy, and increasing labor requirements for the Continental Army. When oppressed persons left the plantation, this caused major social and financial unrest in the colonies. If they formerly held bookings, these defections were even supported by lots of white plantation owners to sign up with the Patriotic cause.

Washington also saw other advantages in Black enlistment. White advanced soldiers just fought in 3-to-4-month increments and returned to their plantations or farms. However, many Black soldiers might serve longer terms. The requirement for the Black soldier was necessary for the war effort, and the requirement to win the war ended up being greater than racist or racial ideology.

Interests assembled with those of innovative Black soldiers as well. When the American nests guaranteed liberty, about a quarter of the Continental Army became Black; before that, more Black folks defected to the British Armed Forces for a possibility to be complimentary. Black revolutionary soldiers comprehended the stakes of the war and understood that they could also leave and benefit from bondage. As historian Gary Nash has said, the Black innovative soldier "can best be comprehended by understanding that his significant commitment was not to a location, not to a people, but to a concept."

Black folks played a dual role - service with the American forces and getting away to the British - both for flexibility. The concept of the Black Patriot is a misused term. In many ways, while the bulk of the whites were battling in the American Revolution, innovative Black soldiers were fighting the "African Americans' Revolution."

Misconception: That enslaved Black and colored Americans didn't have money

Free and enslaved market women dominated local markets, including areas such as Savannah and Charleston, managing networks across the countryside. They made sure fresh materials of fruits, vegetables, and eggs for the marketplaces, as well as a constant flow of money, was available to enslaved folks. Whites described these ladies as "loose" and "disorderly" to criticize their actions as unacceptable behavior for ladies, but white folks of all classes depended on them for survival.

In reality, enslaved people developed financial institutions that specifically shared help to societies. Eliza Allen assisted at least three secret societies for ladies on her own and nearby plantations in Petersburg, Virginia. Cities like Baltimore eventually passed laws against these societies - a sure sign of their popularity. Other cities unwillingly endured them, requiring that a white individual exists at meetings. Enslaved folks, however, discovered imaginative ways to conduct their societies under white folks' noses. Often, the treasurer's ledger listed these members with numbers instead of names so that, when this is discovered, members' identities remained hidden.

During the tumult of the popular Civil War, hundreds of thousands of Black folks looked for haven behind Union lines. Most were impoverished. However, a few managed to bring with them the wealth they had stowed away under beds, in personal chests, and in other concealed places. After the war, Black folks hammered out the Southern Claims Commission for the return of the wealth Union and Confederate soldiers seized or outright stole.

Offered the revival of attention on reparations for slavery and the racial wealth gap, it is very important to remember the long history of Black folks' engagement with the U.S. economy - not just as residential or commercial property, but as savers, spenders, and business people.

Misconception: That Black men were injected with syphilis in the Tuskegee experiment

An unsafe misconception that continues to haunt Black Americans is the belief that the federal government infected about 600 Black men in Macon County, Alabama, with syphilis. This myth has produced generations of African Americans with a healthy suspicion of the American medical occupation. While these men weren't injected with the dangerous syphilis, their story does brighten an essential reality: America's medical past is soaked in racialized terror and the manipulation of Blacks.

"Study of Untreated Syphilis in Black Male" emerged from a research study group formed in 1932 connected with the venereal illness area of the United States Public Health Service. The function of the experiment was to check the effect of syphilis neglected and was conducted at what is now called Tuskegee University, a historically Black university in Macon County, Alabama.

The 600 Black guys in the experiment were not infected with syphilis. Instead, 399 males currently had stages of the disease, and the 201 that did not, acted as a control group. Both groups were kept from treatment of any kind for the 40 years they were observed. The men were subjected to embarrassing and typically painfully intrusive tests and experiments, including spinal taps.

Considered uneducated and impoverished sharecroppers, these males were given free medical exams, hot meals, complementary treatment for small injuries, trips to and from the medical facility, and ensured burial stipends (approximately $50) to be paid to their survivors. The study alongside did not occur through trickery, and numerous African American health workers and teachers associated with the Tuskegee Institute helped in the study.

By the end of the research study in the summer of 1972, after a whistleblower revealed the story in international headlines, only 74 of the guinea pigs were still alive. From the original 399 infected males, 28 had died of syphilis, 100 others from related problems. Forty of the men's spouses had been contaminated, and approximately 19 of their children were born with hereditary syphilis.

As an outcome of the case, the U.S. DHS established the Office for Human Research Protections (OHRP) in 1974 to supervise scientific trials. The case strengthened the concept of African Americans being cast and used as medical guinea pigs.

An unfortunate negative effect of both medical racism and the myth of syphilis injection is that it tangibly reinforces the inability to position trust in the medical system for some African Americans who may pass by to look for help, and as a result, put themselves in danger.

Misconception: That all Black people were shackled until emancipation

One of the most noteworthy misconceptions about the history of Blacks in America is that all were oppressed until the day they were set free. In truth, free biracial neighborhoods existed in Maryland, Louisiana, Virginia, and Ohio long before abolition. For instance, Anthony Johnson, named Antonio the Negro in 1625, was mentioned as a servant. By 1640, he and his better half owned and managed a large plot of land in Virginia.

Some oppressed Africans could sell their labor or craftsmanship to others, making adequate money to buy their liberty. Such is true for Richard Allen, who spent for his freedom in 1786 and co-founded the African Methodist Episcopal Church less than a year later. After the popular American Revolutionary War, Robert Carter III devoted the biggest manumission - or freeing of servants - before Lincoln's Emancipation Proclamation, freeing his 100 shackled Africans.

Not all emancipations were large. Families or people were, in some cases, released upon the death of their enslaver and his family. Many left and lived totally free in the North or Canada. Lastly, generations of children were born in complimentary Black and biracial neighborhoods, many of whom never understood slavery.

Ultimately, slave states established expulsion laws making residency there free of charge unlawful for Black folks. Some submitted petitions to stay near enslaved members of the family, while others moved West or North. And in the Northeast, numerous free Blacks formed benevolent companies such as the Free African Union Society for assistance and, in many cases, repatriation.

The Emancipation Proclamation in 1863 - and the statement of emancipation in Texas two years later - permitted millions of enslaved people to sign up with the ranks of currently complimentary Black Americans.

SECTION FOUR

TALKBACK

CHAPTER V

FAITH

THERE ARE SO MANY WAYS THAT A BLACK MAN CAN TALK back against racism and injustice. It doesn't matter where you are as long as you are not ashamed of it. One of the areas where Blacks are talking back is through their faith. However, to do this in this sphere, you need to understand the role of racism in your faith - where it originated and how it came about.

We are all descendants of Adam and Eve, so all belong and require the redemption offered by Jesus, the Last Adam. From the point of view of the Bible, it is clear that there is one biological race. This is validated by scientific research studies on the human genome. Biblically and biologically, there is no defense of any form of racism. The Black, the white, and the Asian - all colored are all the same.

Have you gone to a shopping center and seen how various people look? There are so many shapes, colors, and sizes. If we all are descendants of Adam and Eve, as the Bible explains, why do we look so different from each other?

The Bible gives us the answers. Adam and Eve are often portrayed to be fair-skinned and blonde; this was unlikely. To obtain all the various skin tones from one couple, we can assume that Adam and Eve most likely were middle-brown in color. Suppose Adam and Eve had a mix of "light color" genes and "dark color" genes. In that case, their descendants might have a broad range of skin color from very light to really dark, with the majority of people somewhere in-between (as seen worldwide today). Adam and Eve most likely possessed genetic variation for eye shape and other identifying qualities.

As a lot of the population migrated from Babel, different groups ended up being separated from others and likely wed only within their language group. Each group brought a set of physical qualities as determined by their genes. As they intermarried, certain qualities would start to dominate due to the group's small pool of genes. Over time, various people groups showed unique physical qualities. For instance, Asians usually have almond-shaped eyes, dark hair, and middle-brown skin, whereas Europeans have round eyes, fair-colored hair, and fair skin.

The term *race* is typically used to classify folks based solely on physical qualities. According to evolutionary ideas, these so-called races came down from various ancestors separated by area and time. Based on scriptural history, the term race needs to be incorrect. We are all one race and from one universal blood.

According to the Bible's history, all people are descendants of Adam and Eve. Thus, just one biological race exists. Today, all humans on the planet are classified as Homo sapiens (exact same genus, species, and subspecies). When the Human Genome Project released a draft of their findings in 2000, the New York Times reported that "the researchers had all declared there is only one race - the mankind."

To form different people groups with distinguishing qualities, one would be required to break up the human population and isolate groups from each other. As written down in Genesis 11, the Tower of Babel provides the historical basis for the development of such folk's groups. There is a lot of detail in the human genome that zillions of combinations are possible.

All people basically have the same skin color - a brown pigment called melanin. A couple of types of melanin and other pigments and elements play minor functions in skin color; every human generally has a brown color.

Lots of brown is called Black; also, a little brown color is called white. In actuality, no human is "Black," and no human is "white." There are not various colors but various tones of one standard color - brown.

While many aspects are associated with figuring out skin color, and the steps are extremely technical, fundamental genes can help us understand the most crucial principles. Assume dominant genes lead to great deals of melanin, and recessive genes lead to little melanin. Adam and Eve were probably a middle brown color with both recessive and dominant genes for the pigment melanin under the skin. Children who received all of the dominant genes would wind up with a lot of the color and be really dark. Kids who received all the recessive genes would end up with only a little color and be really light. Children with a mixture of both recessive and dominant genes would be middle brown.

Naturally, numerous mixes are possible. However, provided that the parents have between them mixes of the recessive and dominant genes, kids might show a large variety of skin shade. With fraternal twins, one twin might acquire genes for lots of melanin while the other could acquire genes for little melanin.

It's not just "Black" and "white." Bottom line: a person's skin shade (what is on the outside) needs to in no way invoke any sort of prejudice or racist remarks. What a distinction we would see in our world if people reacted in accord with scriptural principles, understanding all humans are equivalent before God, and all are sinners in need of redemption. Everybody needs to construct their belief in the outright authority of the Word of God, evaluating all beliefs and mindsets against the clear mentor of what our Creator God teaches us. God advised Samuel of this when He stated, "For the Lord does not see as man sees; for man looks at the outward appearance, but the Lord looks at the heart" (1 Samuel 16:7).

Only One Red Fluid Flows in Us and Holds Our Life

Racism and injustice are a repercussion of sin in a fallen world infused with evolutionary thinking. The consequences of injustice and racism on a social and individual level are big.

Up to this point, we've spent a lot of time looking at historical, scriptural, and scientific reality. By letting the evidence promote itself and translating it through the grid of God's Word, we've discerned some shocking, all-encompassing awareness. Racism is a consequence of man's sin in a fallen world infused with evolutionary thinking. The consequences of bigotry on a social and personal level are huge.

What do we do about it? What do you do about it? We've done enough talking; the time has come for action. In the pages that later follow, we will be taking a look at some individual and very practical application points. Like any real biblical conviction, these actions must begin with a changed heart and an altered understanding of what is real and genuine. In light of what we have discovered, I believe that at least three significant action points remain in order.

Before Darwin, the term "race" was mostly a political and geographical term. People who were carefully associated biologically (such as the English and Irish) were thought to be different races. Darwin's theory has penetrated the whole globe, and the mentor of evolution has redefined the term "race." When many people consider "race," they're considering lower races, greater races, Black races, red races, etc. When we use that term, even the finest of us, at times, have struggled. It simply does not indicate what it used to imply.

Every human remaining in the world is categorized as Homo sapiens. Scientists today concur that there is truly just one biological race of folks. Geneticists have discovered that if we were to take any two folks from anywhere in the world, the fundamental hereditary differences between these two folks would usually be around 0.2 percent, one even if they stemmed from the very same people group. Two "racial" qualities represent just about 6 percent of this 0.2 percent variation. That suggests that the "racial" genetic variation between human beings of different "races" is a simple 0.012 percent.

Overall, there is much more variation within a people group than between one folk group and another. If a Native American individual is trying to find a tissue match for an organ transplant, the very best match may originate from an Asian individual and vice versa. A researcher at the American Association for the Advancement of Science (AAAS) convention in Atlanta in 1997 stated:

"Race is a social construct derived primarily from the perceptions conditioned by the events of taped history, and it has no fundamental biological reality ... curiously enough the concept comes extremely near to being of American manufacture."

The American ABC news science page stated:

"More and more scientists discover that the differences that set us apart are cultural, not racial. Some even state that the word race should be deserted because it's useless ... We accept the concept of race since it's a convenient method of putting people into broad categories, often to suppress them ... the ugliest example is supplied by Hitler's Germany ... Facts actually show that there are differences amongst us, but they originate from culture, not race."

In a 1989 article published in the *Journal of Counseling and Development*, scientists argued that the term "race" is essentially meaningless, which must be disposed of. I agree. Since the impacts of Darwinian evolution and the resulting bias, I think that everybody (and particularly Christians) should abandon the term "race."

The Bible does not even utilize the word "race" in referral to people or man, but it does explain all people as being of one blood. Terms such as these emphasize that we are all associated, from one household, the descendants of the first man. This is the factor Paul states, "All have actually sinned and disappoint the magnificence of God since we are all descendants of Adam." Likewise, Jesus Christ became a descendant of Adam when He came to earth as a male and died as a sacrifice for our sins. He was called the last Adam.

All humans are descendants of Adam; all need to construct their thinking on God's Word and accept that they are sinners in need of redemption; all require to judge their habits in every area, despite the culture, against the absolute requirements of the Word of God; and all require to repent and receive a complimentary gift of salvation.

All of us require to treat everyone as our relative. We all come from one person; we are all equal in value before our Creator God. Any descendant of Adam can be saved since our mutual relative by blood (Jesus Christ) died and rose again. This is why the Gospel can and ought to be preached to all nations and people.

When you are talking to your kids, training them up, and informing them, let's get rid of the word "race." Let us begin to talk about "people groups," and let's speak about how to reach all of them with the good news as Christ commanded.

If each person understood and adopted this scriptural principle, what a distinction it would make in this world! Then each of us might proclaim with Paul, who said, "For there is no distinction between the Jew and Greek: for the exact same Lord over all is abundant unto all that call upon Him" (Romans 10:12).

We Have to Be Reprogrammed in Our Faith

Here's something you might find tough to accept. In the United States culture, we are racially set, particularly regarding the skin color issue. Due to our culture's racist roots, the world believes we have actually been set to take a look at the outside instead of an individual's interior and make broad judgments based on what we see. Had you not been set in that method in this culture, you wouldn't see the differences as you do. Various cultures are set in various methods. Our biases reveal themselves in various methods, but in every case, it is the world and our sinfulness (instead of science and the Bible) that drives our bigotry.

I recognize those are extremely strong words. You might not even agree with me. However, the truth is, it's real. We simply go through our days, making all sorts of presumptions and judgment calls based on external appearances of skin tone, facial functions, size, height, and so on. It's extremely tough to translucent the programs because it appears to be a natural part of the way we believe. Nobody likes to confess it; however, the repercussions are too major to ignore. We've been programmed, and that programming requires change.

This is not a surprise to God, of course. He is completely knowledgeable about the pressures and the influences that the world positions upon us. He likewise specifies clearly that it does not have to stay that way. Modification can happen in our minds and our hearts.

"And do not be conformed to this world, but be transformed by the renewing of your mind, that you may prove what is that good and acceptable and perfect will of God. For I say, through the grace given to me, to everyone who is among you, not to think of himself more highly than he ought to think, but to think soberly, as God has dealt to each one a measure of faith. For as we have many members in one body, but all the members do not have the same function, so we, being many, are one body in Christ, and individually members of one another" (Romans 12:2-6).

If you wish to resolve the issue of bigotry in your own life, it's very simple -- you've got to think the Bible. That's the bottom line. You can invest millions of dollars trying to resolve racist issues. You can pass brand-new laws and institute all sorts of programs; however, unless folks believe the history in the Bible - unless our minds are renewed - we will never have the full image of truth, and we won't have the foundation that we require to make choices that line up with truth instead of the lie.

Everyone should judge our attitudes and our worldviews against the outright authority of the Word of God. Considering our previous performance history, the Church should realize that as a body, we have been highly influenced by the world. Pre-existing worldly biases have highly skewed our interpretation of Scripture. We require to admit where we have been incorrect - and in most cases, we require to repent.

The Church tends to embrace man's ideas and then reinterprets Scripture to fit those preconceived concepts. The result is that the Church is typically conformed to the world rather than changed by the Word. And after that, what occurs? Man modifies his ideas, and the Church has to conform once again. This is what took place with Darwinian development. Many in the Church embraced evolutionary ideas into the Bible; however, now, when it comes to the concern of races, numerous leaders in the world are altering their course. That's great news, but the Church is left in the dust since it compromised the Word of God on the basis of man's previous concepts.

The Church needs to take the lead once again. We require to let the Word promote itself rather than filtering it through worldly and cultural thinking. This indicates that we require to do more than simply say we think the Bible. We need to be scholars of the Bible, "a worker who does not need to be ashamed and who correctly handles the word of truth," as Paul says in 2 Timothy 2:15. Because, to be truthful, the Church has displayed some extremely poor handling of Scripture in order to validate racist presuppositions.

One good example of this is the so-called "curse of Ham." Genesis 9:20-27 records an occurrence including Ham, his son Canaan, and the other boys of Noah, at which time Noah opened his mouth and cursed Canaan. In 1958, Bruce McConkie of the Quorum of the Twelve Apostles stated, "We know the scenarios under which the posterity of Cain (and later on of Ham) was cursed with what we know as Negroid racial characteristics."

This was utilized to justify the pronouncement provided by the church's prophet Brigham Young that stated Blacks would never ever hold the priesthood in the Church of Jesus Christ of Latter-Day Saints. (This "unchangeable" determine of the Prophet was later on rescinded.) In 1929, the Jehovah's Witnesses said, "The curse that Noah pronounced upon Canaan was the origin of the Black race."

However, it's not simply members of the cults that try to use this passage to validate racism. Many folks from mainline Christian denominations have called me on the radio and asked me about the expected "curse of Ham." (Maybe I'm just a tinge extremely delicate to this concern since my name is Ham!) I just ask them to search for the chapter and verse in the Bible. That's constantly the end of that caller because this story states absolutely nothing about skin color or race. Absolutely nothing. It's a basic case of being configured by the world to see something in God's Word that isn't there at all. (And menstruation was on Canaan anyway - not Ham, so my name is clear!).

It's Time to Stand Up in Faith

James 1:22 commands us to be more than simply hearers of the Word. We are to show ourselves "doers of the Word." We are to be people of action. These actions should come from the heart, from the gut, from a figured-out conviction that the problems of racism require us to face it with truth and courage.

Rather than looking at small external distinctions in our physical features or complexion, it's time to look past the reflection of the small portion of our genes and say, "This is my sibling; this is my sibling. I am the same as a person."

It's time to fully learn and use the message that the Lord offered to Samuel. God challenged him to not look at somebody's physical features, skin tone, size, etc. "Do not consider his appearance or his height, for I have rejected him. The Lord does not look at the things people look at" (1 Samuel 16:7). The next time you see anyone who looks slightly different from you, you should ask, "How can I help them? Do they need my love, my care? Do they require the Lord?" We need to treat others as the Lord did. Jesus constantly reached across the undetectable barriers of prejudice to enjoy people, look after folks, and speak truth into people's lives. He connected to touch those who were dirty or those who were pestered with leprosy. He reached throughout ethnic and gender divisions to speak fact into the life of the Samaritan woman at the well (John 4).

If you truly desire to see your life show the life of Christ, then you must begin to enable Christ to love others through you, particularly those who are different than you, simply as He did. You require to start to see as God sees. Whenever you see the European, the Native American, the Arab, the African American, the Asian, the Aborigine, you need to look at them and see your relatives - fellow human beings with the very same values and needs you possess. Just like you, they are seeking affirmation, love, and fact. It's time for you to reveal to them the method you have discovered. Cross the street with your hand outstretched, prepared to shake the hand of another shade of melanin. Be willing to cross to "the opposite of the tracks" to fellow-ship and worship as a unified and diverse body.

Due to your programming by the world and by evolutionary think-ing, these acts will need conscious options - options based upon fact and the clear teaching of Scripture utilizing Christ as your design and your strength. In time, you'll discover that you are no longer being adhered to the world; however, you are transformed by renewing your mind. Instead of seeing differences, you will see those from a different folk's group, and right away think, *they're my family members!*

As the love of Jesus Christ begins to stir within your soul, God will show you what to do. You will make the option, and you will act. However, it will actually be Christ enjoying them through you. Whether it is in big leaps or little actions, God can utilize you to bridge the so-called "racial barriers" that have actually been made in our minds through both worldly thinking and evolutionary philosophy.

It will surely make an enormous difference in the lives around you as you start to act that method and think! What a distinction it will make in the world as increasingly more people use up this cause! We are recovering Darwin's garden for Christ. By picking to act, we take out the weeds of evolutionary thought and replant with seeds of truth, love, empathy, and understanding. That's what it's all about.

What Constitutes a "Race"?

In the 1800s, before Darwinian advancement became popularized, many people, when talking about "races," would be describing such groups as the "English race," "Irish race," and so on. This all increased in 1859 when Charles Darwin released his book *On the subject of Origin of Species by Means of Mutual Selection or the Preservation of Favoured Races in the Struggle for Life.*

Darwinian evolution was (and still is) inherently a racist philosophy, teaching that different groups or "races" of people developed at different times, so some groups are more like their apelike descendants than others. Leading evolutionist, Stephen Jay Gould, claimed that "biological arguments for bigotry may have been typical before 1859, but they increased by numbers following the acceptance of the evolutionary theory."

The Australian Aborigines, for instance, were thought to be the missing links between the apelike forefather and the rest of humanity. This led to horrible prejudices and injustices towards the Australian Aborigines.

Racist mindsets fueled by evolutionary thinking were mainly

accountable for an African pygmy being shown with a monkey in a cage in the Bronx Zoo. Congo pygmies were once believed to be "little apelike, elfish creatures" that "exhibit many ape-like features in their bodies.".

As an outcome of Darwinian advancement, many people began believing in terms of the various people groups worldwide representing different "races," however, within the context of the evolutionary viewpoint. This has led to many people today, purposely or unconsciously, having instilled bias against specific groups of people.

All people in the world today are categorized as Homo sapiens. Researchers today confess that, biologically, there really is only one race of human beings. For instance, a researcher at the Advancement of Science Convention in Atlanta specified, "Race is a social construct obtained mainly from perceptions conditioned by events of documented history, and it has no fundamental biological truth." This individual went on to state, "Curiously enough, the concept comes very close to being of American manufacture.".

Reporting on a research study carried out on the concept of race, ABC News mentioned, "More and more scientists find that the distinctions that set us apart are not racial but cultural. Some are even of the notion that the word race should be abandoned since it's useless." The short article went on to state that "we accept the concept of the race since it's a practical way of putting folks into broad categories, frequently to reduce them - the ugliest example was provided by Hitler's Germany. And racial bias stays common throughout the world."

More recently, those dealing with mapping the human genome announced: "that they had actually put together a draft of the whole sequence of the human genome, and the scientists had all stated, there is only one race - the human race.".

Personally, because of the impacts of Darwinian advancement and the resulting bias, I think everybody (and particularly Christians) must abandon the term "race(s)." We might refer rather to the various "folk's groups" worldwide.

Skin Color in Faith

When Jesus stated, "Let the little children come to me, and do not hinder them, for the kingdom of heaven belongs to such as these" (Matthew 19:14). He did not identify skin colors. In reality, scientists have found that there is one major pigment, called melanin, that produces our skin color. There are two main types of melanin: eumelanin (brown to black) and pheomelanin (red to yellow). These combine to offer us the specific shade of skin that we have.

Melanocytes produce melanin. These are cells in the bottom layer of the skin. No matter what our shade of skin, all of us have roughly the very same concentration of melanocytes in our bodies. Melanocytes insert melanin into melanosomes, which move the melanin into other skin cells, dividing (stem cells) mainly in the most affordable layer of the skin.

In the stem cells, the pigment produces its function as it forms a little dark umbrella over each nucleus. The melanin protects the skin cells from being harmed by sunlight. In folks with lighter skin tones, much of the pigment is lost after these cells divide, and their child cells move up in the skin to form the surface's dead layer - the stratum corneum.

Geneticists have discovered that four to six genes, each with numerous alleles (or variations), manage the quantity and kind of melanin produced. A large variety of skin tones exist because of this. In reality, it is rather simple for one couple to produce a vast array of skin shades in simply one generation, as will be revealed listed below.

Our Inheritance

DNA (deoxyribonucleic acid) is the molecule of genetics that is passed from parents to children. In human beings, the child acquires 23 chromosomes from each parent (the daddy contributes 23 through his sperm, while the mother contributes 23 through her egg). At the moment of conception, these chromosomes join to form a special combination of DNA and control much of what makes the kid an individual. Each chromosome set includes numerous genes, which manage the physical development of the kid. Keep in mind that no brand-new hereditary information is produced at conception, but a new combination of already existing hereditary information is formed.

To illustrate the basic genetic principles associated with figuring out skin shade, we'll utilize a simplified explanation, with simply two genes managing the production of melanin. Let's state that the A and B versions of the genes account for a lot of melanin, and the a and b variations account for a small quantity of melanin.

If the father's sperm brought the AB version and the mom's ovum carried the AB, the offspring would be AABB, with a lot of melanin, and therefore very dark skin. If both parents carry the ab variation, the kid would be aabb, with very little melanin, and thus extremely light skin. If the daddy carries AB (very dark skin) and the mother carries ab (really light skin), the offspring will be AaBb, with a middle brown shade of skin. The bulk of the world's population has a middle brown skin shade.

An easy exercise with a Punnet Square reveals that if each parent has a middle brown shade of skin (AaBb), they might produce a result in a wide range of skin tones in just one generation. Based upon the skin colors seen today, we can deduce that Adam and Eve most likely would have had a mid-brown skin color. Their children, and even grandchildren, could have ranged from really light to really dark.

Nobody truly has red, or yellow, or Black skin. All of us have the very same fundamental color, simply different shades of it. We all share the very same pigments - our bodies just have various combinations of them.

Melanin likewise identifies eye color. In the situation when the eye has a larger amount of melanin, it will be brown. The eye will be blue if the iris has a little melanin. (The blue color in blue eyes emanates from the method light scatters off the thin layer of brown-colored melanin.).

Hair color is also affected by the production of melanin. Brown to Black hair arises from a higher production of melanin, while lighter hair results from less melanin. Those with red hair have an anomaly in one gene that causes a higher percentage of the reddish type of melanin (pheomelanin) to be produced.

DNA likewise controls the basic shape of our eyes. Those whose DNA codes for an extra layer of fat around the eyes have almond-shaped eyes (this prevails amongst Asian folk's groups). All folk's groups have adipose tissue around the eyes; some just have more or less than normal.

Origin of People Groups

People with darker skin tend to live in warmer environments, while those with lighter skin tend to live in cooler environments. Why are certain features more prominent in some parts of the world?

We all know for sure that Adam and Eve were the first two people. Their descendants filled the earth. Nevertheless, the world's population was lowered to eight throughout the Flood of Noah. From these eight people have come all the people and nations. It is most likely that the skin shade of Noah and his household was middle brown. This would allow his children and their spouses to produce various skin tones in simply one generation. Barriers that may have prohibited their descendants from freely intermarrying weren't as terrific as they are today because there was a typical language, and everyone lived in the very same general vicinity. Hence, distinct differences in features and skin color in the population weren't as prevalent as they are today.

In Genesis 11, we read of the disobedience at the Tower of Babel. God judged this rebellion by giving each family group a different language. This made it exceedingly difficult for the groups to comprehend each other; therefore, they split apart, each extended family going its own method and finding a different location to live. The outcome was that the people were scattered over the earth.

Since the new language and geographical barriers, the groups no longer easily mixed with other groups, and the outcome was splitting the gene pool. Different cultures formed with certain features ending up being primary within each group. The characteristics of each became a growing number as new generations of kids were born. If we were to go back in time to Babel and blend the folks into entirely various household groups, then people groups with entirely various characteristics may result. For instance, we may discover a fair-skinned group with tight, curly dark colored hair that has blue, almond-shaped eyes. Or a group with much darker skin, blue eyes, and straight brown hair.

Some of these (skin color, eye shape, and so on) became basic attributes of each specific folk's group through numerous choice pressures (environmental, sexual, and so on) and/or anomaly. For example, since of the protective aspect of melanin, those with darker skin would have been more likely to make it through in areas where sunshine is more intense (warmer, tropical areas near the equator), as they are less likely to suffer from illness such as skin cancer. Those with much lighter skin lack the melanin needed to protect them from the damaging UV rays. So, they might have been most likely to pass away before the ability to reproduce. UVA radiation likewise damages the B vitamin folate, which is needed for DNA synthesis in cellular division. Low levels of folate present in pregnant women can cause defects in the developing baby. Again, because of this, lighter-skinned people may have been affected in areas of extreme sunlight.

On the other hand, melanin works as a natural sunblock, restricting the sunlight's ability to promote the liver to produce vitamin D, helping the body soak up calcium and construct strong bones. Given that those with darker skin need more sunlight to produce vitamin D, they may not have been as able to endure in areas of less sunshine (northern, cooler regions) as their lighter-skinned member of the family, who do not need as much sunshine to produce appropriate quantities of vitamin D. Those who did not have vitamin D are more most likely to develop diseases such as rickets (which is connected with a calcium shortage), which can trigger slowed development and bone fractures. It is understood that when those with darker skin lived in England during the Industrial Revolution, they were more prone to establish rickets because of the basic absence of sunshine.

Naturally, these are generalities. Exceptions happen, such as in the case of the darker-skinned Inuit people residing in cold northern regions. Their food consists of fish, the oil of which is a good source of vitamin D, which might account for their survival in this location.

Genuine science in the present fits with the scriptural view that all people are rather closely associated - there is just one race biologically. For that reason, to go back to our initial question, there is, in essence, no such thing as interracial marriage. We are left with this: is there anything in the Bible that speaks clearly against men and women from diverse groups wedding?

The Separation at Babel

Keep in mind that the context of Genesis 11 clarifies that the reason for God's scattering the folks over the earth was that they had unified in rebellion against Him. Some Christians indicate this occasion in an effort to offer a basis for their arguments versus so-called interracial marriage. They believe that this passage suggests that God is stating that folks from various folk's groups can't wed so that the countries are kept apart. There is no such sign in this passage that "interracial marital relationship" is condemned. Besides, there has been a lot of blending of folk's groups over the years that it would be difficult for every human being today to trace their family tree back to understand from which specific group(s) they are descended.

We require to comprehend that the sovereign developer God supervises the countries of this world. Apostle Paul makes this clear in Acts 17:26. Some people erroneously declare this verse to imply that folks from different countries shouldn't marry. This passage has nothing to do with a marital relationship. As John Gill makes clear in his timeless commentary, the context is that God is in charge of all things - where, how, and for how long any people, person, or country will live, flourish, and die.

Even with this, God is working to win for Himself a people who are one in Christ. The Bible explains in Galatians 3:28, Colossians 3:11, and Romans 10:12-13 that there is no distinction between male or female or Jew or Greek regarding redemption. In Christ, any separation between folks is broken down. As believers, we are one in Christ and thus have a common purpose - to live for Him who made us. This oneness in Christ is essential to comprehending marital relationships.

CHAPTER VI
FAMILY

WHEN WE TALK ABOUT TALKING BACK THROUGH THE family, we don't only mean discussing racism with your parents, children, or other siblings; it includes joining and supporting groups such as the NAACP.

Several factors contribute to the degradation of the Black community, which leads to instability in the country.

Fathers have an essential role to play in the social development of their children.

A father who is involved in and accountable for his children's actions as they grow, these fathers strengthen their kids' behavioral advancement beginning in infancy and lasting through teenage and adult years. Kids are a lot more socially and mentally developed when their dads are included. They are more understanding, have much better friendships, and better deal with disappointment and racial pressure. The kids whose fathers are present are more likely to have a more sustained mentality when they grow to become adults. A father's involvement can also go a long way towards preventing racial outbursts in teenage years.

Research study about a mother's function in a young child's development is widely publicized, mainly because the attachment theory gives a basis for performing the research. No such theory exists for father figures, which might belong to why the influence dads have on their children wasn't also researched until recently when scientists started to move far from looking at dads as the "other moms and dad."

The father and mother are the two dearest and most important people in the life of every child. We can suppose the role of the mother is clear to everyone. In that case, the father's role is often unconscious, incomprehensible, and, to our great regret, often comes down to only punishments in the life of a little man. In the meantime, our children so desperately need their father's participation in their lives - his friendship, care, and protection.

There is a well-established theory that the most important thing for a child's behavioral development is the mother-child bond. But it turns out that communication between a child and the father is no less important for the full formation of his social personality. So why is the role of the father usually considered secondary? Studies have shown that 7 out of 10 people believe that the mother and father have equal responsibility for raising a child. But in reality, fathers spend less than one month a year with their children on average. But it has long been known that children growing up without a father learn slower and have lower self-esteem.

Moreover, such children are much more likely to commit social crimes. After all, every baby needs harmonious development, which can only be obtained with both parents. Mom gives her child tenderness and affection, father - protection, confidence, and character.

Experts note that it is quite difficult to grow a full-fledged personality, whether it be a boy or a girl, without male influence. No one denies the possibility of success in parenting without a father. Still, as life has proven over the years, this is the truth. After all, it depends on both parents to determine how their children will grow to influence society.

So how can a modern father be involved in raising a child to tackle this racial society?

In the first year of life, the father's role in the child's physical development and the formation of basic motor skills are incredibly significant. As a rule, the games of dads with children are different from how mothers entertain babies: fathers are more inclined to active physical amusements; they are not afraid to toss children, twirl them, teach them to somersault, roll on their shoulders, etc. This stimulates the little ones to be physically active. It is from this that the child understands that he should be protective of his weaker friends.

The father can become an invaluable aid in the development of the child's thinking. It is observed that fathers can teach children how to speak and the right words to say when under pressure.

The father teaches the child to adequately perceive the social hierarchy (subordination and accountability). He makes him understand what authority means, introduces such social instruments as approval and or punishment. This is because, unlike the mother, who loves the child simply because he "is," the father usually makes certain demands on the child that he must meet.

The father is the embodiment of discipline, standards, and norms. This balance of acceptance (mom) and giving (dad) is essential for personal development.

The dad is responsible for the child's acceptance of his gender, race, and the assimilation of the appropriate model of behavior.

Fathers and son: Fathers always try to raise real men from their sons, but sometimes this good intention translates into detachment. Excessive discipline may develop into fear and abuse.

Father and daughter: It is the father who determines the destiny of his daughter. Her success in her personal life, the choice of partners and relationships, and how she sees society.

Some years back, Kweisi Mfume and the president of the NAACP were interviewed. Two questions were asked, "As between the presence of white racism and the absence of Black fathers, the questions were asked, "Which poses the bigger threat to the Black community?" Instantly Kweisi Mfume said, "The absence of Black fathers." Considering what President Obama said… "We all know the statistics. That child who grows up without a father is five times more likely to live in poverty and commit a crime; 9 times more likely to drop out of school, and 20 times more likely to end up in prison." *The Journal of Research on Adolescence* confirms this statement that even after controlling for varying household income levels, kids in father-absent homes are more prone to end up in jail. And kids who never in their lives had a father in the house are the most susceptible to wind up behind bars.

In 1960, five percent of America's children entered the world without a mother and father married to each other. By 1980, it was 18 percent; by 2000, it had risen to 33 percent; 15 years after that, the number reached 41 percent, and that number is still growing to date.

For Blacks, even during the slavery period, when marriage for slaves was illegalized, Black children were more likely when compared to today to be raised by both their mother and father. The famous economist Walter Williams has written that, according to census data, from 1890 to 1940, a Black child was more likely to grow up with married parents than a white child.

For Blacks, out-of-wedlock births had gone from 25 percent in 1965 to 73 percent in 2015 and from far less than 5 percent to way over 25 percent for whites. Also, for Hispanics, out-of-wedlock births have risen to 53 percent.

WHAT HAPPENED TO FATHERS?

The answer is found in a basic economics law. If you subsidize undesirable behavior, you will get more undesirable behavior. In 1949, the nation's poverty rate was 34 percent. By 1965, it was cut in half to 17 percent - all before President Lyndon Johnson's so-called War on Poverty. But after that war began in 1965, poverty began to flat line. From 1965 until now, the government has spent over $20 trillion to fight poverty.

The poverty rate has remained unchanged, but the relationship between poor men and women has changed - dramatically. That's because our generous welfare system allows women, in effect, to marry the government. And this makes it all too easy for men to abandon their traditional moral and financial responsibilities. Psychologists call such dependency "learned helplessness."

How do we know that the welfare state creates disincentives that hurt the very people we are trying to help? They tell us. In 1985, the Los Angeles Times asked both the poor and the non-poor whether poor women "often" have children to get additional benefits. Most of the non-poor respondents said no. However, 64 percent of poor respondents said yes.

Now, who do you think is in a better position to know?

Tupac Shakur, the late rapper, once said: "I know for a fact that had I had a father, I'd have some discipline. I'd have more confidence." He admitted he began running with gangs because he wanted the things a father gives to a child, especially to a boy: structure and protection. "Your mother cannot calm you down the way a man can," Shakur said. "You need a man to teach you how to be a man."

NAACP Family

NAACP is an abbreviation of the National Association for the Advancement of Coloured People and was founded in 1909 in New York City. It is known as the oldest, largest, and strongest Civil Rights organization in the United States. The NAACP's principal goal is to guarantee the political, instructional, social, and financial equality of minority people in the United States. I have understood the organization's presence and have heard about some of its contributions. I was rather unfamiliar with particular information about this organization. From my previous research studies of African Americans and subjects and books, I have frequently become aware of the NAACP, so I constantly sought the chance to discover out more information about this group. For that reason, this assignment was a fantastic chance for me. Since I had no concept of which book I must try to find to examine the NAACP, I used the internet to get the info. The NAACP has an efficient site with details about its history, existing activities, and even a subscription application. Through the search, I learned several new things that shocked me.

I had related to the NAACP as an organization just for African

Americans because this organization focuses on Civil Rights. The Civil Rights Movement only describes African Americans and no other minorities. This is completely my misconception. The word "minority" consists of all ethnic groups that seek a level playing field and rights in this nation. I changed from my ignorance; however, it was genuinely good to correct my misperception.

The next thing which overwhelmed me was the variety of its branches. The NAACP is a network of over 2,200 branches covering all 50 states. The NAACP serves folks at the local level by responding to the requirement of citizens for action on concerns. The NAACP has branches, even in Japan. The Los Angeles Chapter is among the branches. It was formed in 1914 by Drs. John and Vada Somerville, both graduates of the University of Southern California and active leaders in the affairs of the Black community. The focus of this is opposing racial discrimination and second-class treatment of the city's colored or Black folks and working as the principal political management in the Black neighborhood. The advantage the NAACP offers the community is clear, particularly around the theme of education. For instance, in 1932, in the aftermath of an earthquake that damaged Los Angeles public schools, the branch filed an effective suit versus the Monrovia School Board to force them to provide Black trainees with the very same opportunity as white trainees who were allowed to enlist because city's schools up until Los Angeles schools might reopen. Today, the branch still supports the programs and policies of the NAACP with aggressive action at the local level.

NAACP is devoted to accomplishment through nonviolence and trusts journalism, the petition, the court, and the ballot, and is persistent in using moral and legal persuasion. In my viewpoint, this attitude provides kids with a design demonstrating how minorities can combat inequality.

Lawyer's Committee for Civil Rights Under Law

The Lawyer's Committee is a nonpartisan, nonprofit organization that was formed in 1963 at the demand of President John F. Kennedy to include the private bar in offering legal services to resolve racial discrimination. The Committee's significant goal is to utilize the bar's skills and resources to acquire an equivalent chance for minorities by dealing with aspects that contribute to racial justice and economic change. Given our country's history of racial discrimination, de jure partition, and the de facto injustices that continue, the Lawyers' Committee's main focus is to represent the interest of African Americans especially, other ethnic and racial minorities, and other victims of discrimination, where doing so can assist in protecting justice for all racial and ethnic minorities.

NAACP Legal Defense and Educational Fund

For more than half a century, LDF has utilized the law as an effective tool to pry open doors of opportunity long near African Americans, other folks of color, and females.

This Legal Defense and Educational Fund, Inc. (LDF or, simultaneously, the "Inc. Fund") supplies legal services in the fight against racial discrimination. The NAACP program for reform had long combined legal difficulties to de jure partition and disfranchisement with public campaigns such as anti-lynching legislation and expanded academic chances. However, increasing pressure from the Internal Revenue System (IRS) in the 1930s required the NAACP to develop a separate LDF in 1940. It runs independently today as part of ongoing resistance against racism in the United States.

The NAACP's public campaigns versus lynching in the 1920s drew increasing attention to the value of fundraising and lobbying within the company's mission of difficult Jim Crow inequalities. In 1925, the IRS initially rejected the right of donors to the NAACP to claim tax deductions on their federal income tax. This policy was enhanced in 1934 and 1938 on the grounds that the NAACP's program was political, not charitable or instructional. Concerned that this would prevent donations to the NAACP, nationwide leaders supported the facility of a separate "legal wing" under Thurgood Marshall's leadership, championing the LDF as a partner to the NAACP itself.

Until the 1950s, the LDF and NAACP operated in tandem regardless of emerging tensions over management and focus. LDF attorneys shared the NAACP office in the early 1940s, and officials typically served flexibly within both organizations. The LDF has taken advantage of association with the recognized NAACP, yet NAACP and LDF personnel sometimes clashed as competitors over fundraising for various causes and specific techniques focused on challenging racial inequalities in the country's courts.

These tensions expanded after Marshall's success in the case of Brown v. Board of Education (1954), which officially overturned the Plessy choice. Southern states reacted to the special Supreme Court decision with various stalling tactics and crackdowns on companies promoting combination and racial reform. Lawyers related to the NAACP and the LDF were threatened with charges of unlawfully or unethically drumming up legal service in their pursuit of executing the Brown choice, while NAACP chapters were directed to sign up all members and contributors with the state, methods planned to break down both companies' ability to run in the South. By 1957 the LDF concurred officially to separate from the NAACP, wishing to conserve legal energies and protect financial resources from attack. The separation financially benefitted the LDF as public interest in the Brown cases brought increasing contributions to the legal organization while the NAACP discovered itself relying more greatly on membership fees for financial survival.

The LDF continues to act as a legal advocate for African American equality in the United States, working to support civil liberties gains made in the 1960s, such as the Civil Rights Act of 1964 and the Voting Rights Act of 1965, in addition to highlighting racial inequalities in our justice system.

National Urban League

The National Urban League is the country's oldest and biggest community-based movement dedicated to empowering African Americans to get into the financial and social mainstream.

National Urban League, an American service firm, was established to remove racial segregation and discrimination and assist African

Americans and other minorities to take part in all stages of American life. At the ending of the 20th century, over 110 local associated groups were active throughout the United States. It is headquartered in New York City.

The Urban League traces its roots to 3 organizations -the Committee for the Improvement of Industrial Conditions Among Black Americans in New York (founded in 1906), the National League for the Protection of Coloured Women (founded 1906), and the Committee on Urban Conditions Among Negroes (established 1910) - that combined in 1911 to form the National League on Urban Conditions Among Negroes. The brand-new organization looked to help African Americans, particularly those relocating to New York City from rural places in the South (see Great Migration), to discover jobs, real estate, and normally get used to metropolitan life. The design of the organization established in New York City was imitated in other cities where affiliates were quickly established. By 1920, the national company had presumed the much shorter name, National Urban League.

From its start, the league has been interracial; the company's real facility was led by George Edmund Haynes, the very first African American to receive a Ph.D. from Columbia University, and Ruth Standish Baldwin, who was a white New York City philan-thropist. The Urban League's primary task of assisting migrants gradually evolved over the years into bigger issues. The organization highlighted work rights for African Americans during the director-ship of Eugene Kinkle Jones (1918-41); and his successor, Lester Granger (1941-61), highlighted tasks for African Americans in the defense industry and tried to breach the color barrier common in labor unions throughout World War II. During the rule of Whitney M. Young, Jr. (1961-71), the league became among the strongest forces in the American civil liberties battle. Under his follower, Vernon E. Jordan, Jr. (1971-81), the league widened its vision by accepting such causes as environmental security, energy conserva-tion, and the basic problems of poverty. The league's ideals at the turn of the 21st century included the idea of achievement as it connects to racial identity, global issues such as globalization and its economic results on the African American neighborhood, and education.

Fitness

From helping people lose weight to preventing chronic illness, getting fit has lots of advantages. With the ideal exercise, you can extend the benefits beyond yourself to help the fellow neighbor by using it to fight racism. Here are some methods that will help you talk back.

Help a Furry Companion

Whether you are searching for an excuse to get out for a walk or run, go to your local animal or humane shelter. These companies often look for volunteers who want to walk or run canines that are seeking homes. Many of these canines are active and require time playing or running outside beyond what routine volunteers can offer. This uses a fantastic strategy to survive a run while making a good friend in the process. Depending upon your physical fitness level, you will be assigned dogs with various activity levels. In this process, you can meet people and find opportunities to discuss racial injustice.

Running for This Cause

Raising funds to treat cancer to feeding those in need, racing for a cause gives you additional rewards to train and run. Whether you are training for a 2km or a marathon, your miles give you a chance to get in shape and, in turn, assist in raising funds for people in need.

Depending on people's race or color, you can take the effort to raise funds on your own, just like you would when working in a Team in Training; with this, you can create awareness about racism. Try to get people of different colors involved.

Donate Your Miles

Whether you walk, run, or bike, you can contribute your miles to fighting racism and injustice by utilizing an app on your phone. For instance, Charity Miles enables you to track your miles by starting the app when you start your exercise. Determine which charity you wish to support, with choices including the Stand Up to Cancer, ASPCA, and Wounded Warrior Project. With this, you can begin your own "stand against racism and injustice" charity organization.

Host an Outdoor Physical Fitness Event

Take all the advantages of regional public spaces and warmer weather to get your members - and the public - outdoors. In Boston, several local health clubs - including IHRSA members like Health-works - have led physical fitness classes outdoors as a vital part of the Boston Public Health Commission's "Summer Fitness Series" effort to get more people moving during warmer months. This brings unity between people of different colors.

Support A Local Charitable Cause

Open your club up to those around you and your community and contribute the earnings to a local charity. ACAC in Charlottesville, VA, has achieved success with a "25 days for $25" design, in which neighborhood members pay $25 for 25 days of subscription at the club. Under this typical model, club traffic doubled, and 33% of participants signed up with the club following the promo. This is used to talk about racial injustice.

Exhibition at a Health Fair

Numerous corporations are concerned about their employees' health, as much healthier employees are typically more productive and sustain fewer healthcare costs. Offer to run a table at a business health fair, where you can offer fitness and health tests and promote the services your club could supply to their workers. Events like this are also a terrific location to expand unique programs for non-members and discuss racism and injustice against Blacks.

Go on Local Radio

Showcase your know-how by offering to go on a regional radio program and discuss physical activity and health. Speak about the programs at your club, any upcoming neighborhood events, and the benefits of exercise, and how it will reduce racial injustice.

There are many social advantages of physical activity. Confidence is essential to a good social life; exercise assists with that. As you end up being more powerful and much faster, your self-confidence will grow, you'll have the ability to take pride in the physical things you can now do and value the development you've made.

Physical activity can likewise assist your concentration skills by providing a release valve for stress and pressure and encouraging higher endorphins levels. You'll be happier in general if you can concentrate well on essential work and social tasks.

Being social is most satisfying when you feel great about yourself, have a favorable self-image, and high self-confidence. Exercise can aid with that. By keeping a healthy weight and an uplifted state of mind, you'll feel better about yourself and regularly participate in social activities.

One of the most significant social benefits of a workout is simply that - an improved social life. If you take part in team sports or workout with a group, you'll develop higher compassion and social abilities. You'll also make good new friends and get brand-new social outlets.

Among the first places folks look when it comes to looking at these social benefits that exercise needs to offer come from inspiration. A lot of us struggle to stick to a workout plan. Whether you get hectic or get bored, there are tons of reasons out there to explain why people quit. Working out with a friend is among one of the best ways to give you a substantial push to keep you going.

Furthermore, self-confidence is another element that social exercise can benefit from, specifically if you're new to it. Getting into the fitness center or starting a new workout for the first time can be difficult. Having someone else there that has got your back can extremely make all the difference. No matter if you're signing up with a sports group, hitting the gym together, or just talking about in-home exercises, it can truly assist when you know you're not alone.

Taking things into a more favorable light, working out with others can be an awesome method to make things more fun, too. Increased drive isn't the only benefit you get from working out. Having another person there with you to talk to and make progress with can make things way more fun than a solo workout. Take our word for it!

If another person's presence isn't quite adequate for you to keep pressing on, competition certainly can be. Making competition is simple if you're working out with a friend or friends or even playing in a group. See who can hit their objectives initially, raise the most weight, do the most reps, score the most goals, whatever you like. Making a game out of it can truly get the adrenaline building, and that can press you more than anything if you enjoy it.

If you have the opportunity to work out with somebody more knowledgeable than you, or perhaps in a group, that alone can open brand-new doors and see new benefits that you never even knew or imagined you needed from social exercise. Having someone who understands more than you is the best method to discover new and much better benefits. Whether it's a brand-new exercise or a much better method, a sensible training buddy or colleague can be a genuine game-changer if you're ready to discover and support each other.

On a smaller scale, workout partners do a remarkably similar sort of thing (not to be confused with exercising with your partner, unless that is your workout partner). You will more than likely discover your exercise routines more satisfying when developing a constant group of workout partners or even just one training friend. The psychological support from motivating each other to push further or increase the weight is a boost alone. It offers you a psychological edge that you may not have already had and can be a game-changer in the brief and long term.

You also have that physical support that working out in a group needs to use, with them being able to mention any threats or defects in your workout methods that you might not have even noticed or could see. In addition, they would also have the ability to spot you while you experiment with a much heavier load than you could on your own and do so safely.

Folks enjoy playing and training with sporting clubs and playing games on weekends, or perhaps weeknights. It makes the workout more enjoyable, but it also provides you with something to do with your leisure time and a possibility to complete it if that's what you like doing. It's all relative, and it's all friendly!

This indicates that not only can you take encouragement from your pals and share your personal goal accomplishments, but you can likewise learn things from other people and watch how they are training. There are even online forums and message boards that you can participate in to make certain you can get the info you need while still having the ability to assist others and make new buddies along the way.

CHAPTER VII

FINANCE

RACISM, INJUSTICE AGAINST BLACKS, AND OTHER KINDS OF discrimination against minorities are, unfortunately, typical phenomena throughout history and in current times. The Black Lives Matter movement and the protests that followed the murder of George Floyd in Minneapolis, United States, highlight that lots of Americans consider discrimination a major issue in the nation today.

Discrimination is very upsetting to people from targeted minorities. However, as we demonstrated, the results of leaving out talented people from financial opportunities tend to go further. When society discriminates against a specific group, its entire economy can suffer.

In 1932, Jews held around 15 percent of senior managerial positions in German companies listed on the Berlin Stock Exchange. When these top supervisors were tossed out, the business was not able to change them adequately. New senior management groups at the affected business were less linked to other businesses, less educated, and had less supervisory experience. The stock rates and profitability of the afflicted business decreased sharply after 1933, compared to unaffected companies. These results were distinct from other shocks hitting German business after 1933, for instance, policies by the Nazi federal government or changes in demand for companies' products.

The cumulative effects of losing Jewish managers were big: an approximate calculation suggests that the marketplace evaluation of business noted in Berlin fell by almost two percent of German gross national product. Besides being drastic, the impacts were persistent. The performance of afflicted companies did not recover for a minimum of 10 years, the end of our sample duration. This suggests that the increase of an inequitable ideology can result in persistent and first-order financial losses.

There are essential distinctions between the 1930s example of antisemitism in action and what many Black Americans face today. A history of slavery and bigotry has made it more challenging for Black Americans to reach management positions. However, just as in Nazi Germany, these aspects have an economic cost. Barriers such as limited access to education might have avoided an optimal allotment of skill.

Impacts of racism on finance

1. *It stifles imagination.*

Variety is proven to increase development and, as a result, business' monetary efficiency. As a European Institute for Managing Diversity report notes, it can help firms move away from "minimal unilateral thinking" and help them discover brand-new items, markets, and ways of managing an organization.

The monetary benefits might be substantial. In the UK alone, complete BAME representation in an organization, particularly management roles, could be worth £ 24 billion ($30 billion). Businesses that do badly on diversity, though, can anticipate doing badly or completely stop. A McKinsey report on the subject discovered the businesses that performed worst on variety were nearly 30% more likely to underperform on success.

Suppose they're going to be completely engaged and bring their finest concepts to work. In that case, it's important that employees from underrepresented groups feel protected in their offices. Specialists say "psychologically safe" employees are more likely to be thinking about finding excellence and connecting with others than simply looking great to their companies.

2. A poisonous work culture is no good for anybody.

On the flip side, a company that appears to tolerate racist behavior creates a lack of psychological security for its employees. This leads to disengagement, lower productivity, and higher personnel turnover.

It's an issue that continues and, around the world, stories of discrimination and bullying continue to be reported. For example, in the United States, most Black workers state they have experienced racism at work. And, as one guy informed Fortune, the issue can become more noticeable the further up the ladder folks climb.

These biases exist in the employing process. One Danish research study, released in the *American Economic Journal*, found that personal predispositions result in people selecting coworkers of the very same ethnic background even if they are less efficient foregoing 8% of their earnings at the same time.

3. It increases absenteeism and health concerns amongst employees.

When people experience this type of discrimination at work, it can impact their psychological and physical health.

According to a research study from the United States National Institute for Health, racial discrimination and workplace bullying can lead people to smoke or drink heavily as a coping mechanism. But it does not stop there. The resulting stress, the report states, can result in a boost in problems like obesity, high blood pressure, and anxiety. Disadvantageous behaviors like leaving work early, arriving late, or not completing a task on time typically follow.

Less overt kinds of discrimination take their toll, too. More subtle types consist of things like someone being unfairly overlooked for a promotion or being pushed into early retirement. In all, when discrimination is extensive, trust declines, and spirits throughout the company drop.

Structural racism likewise leads to lower wages for Black folks and even more so for Black females. Colored or Black people are paid less in the United States, for example - guys 13% less and ladies 21% less. This wage inequality results in hardship and restricted access to healthcare. In the United States, the hardship rate for African American women is nearly twice that of white women.

4. It results in bad PR, loss of income, and litigation.

All of this impacts how a business is seen by those outside of the company. Employees are among a company's greatest potential supporters, and when workers aren't delighted, they get the word out.

This might lead to profit loss as people and companies among employees' personal networks prevent working with the business. And it might hurt recruitment efforts, too, as job seekers investigating the business are likely to look somewhere else if they reveal a service that does not appear to support their values. Recent research studies show 70% of job seekers now desire to work for a firm that promotes diversity and inclusion.

Add to all this the truth that racial discrimination violates the law in many nations, and a business bogged down in a high-profile legal case might find they have to pay substantial damages. Again, that's simply the financial expense. The reputational damage to the company could be considerable.

5. People want to work with firms that take an anti-racist method

According to an Edelman report, this is the bottom line, and it affects the service bottom line, too: 64% of consumers internationally will purchase from or boycott a brand based upon its position on a social or political problem.

A more recent Edelman poll, performed after George Floyd's death in the United States, discovered that Americans anticipate brands to play an essential part in attending to systemic bigotry: 60% said they would purchase from or boycott a brand name based on its response to the Floyd demonstrations. This figure rose to 70% for the 18-34 age group.

People do not simply desire brand names to speak out - they want them to act. The majority of the study participants required businesses to utilize marketing budget plans to inform the public on racial equality by taking on the source of the issue and addressing variety in their own companies, communications, and items.

Long-lasting dedication

Services have an ethical obligation to resolve this issue, of course. But when the influence on companies that do not act is considered, it is clear that embracing an anti-racist technique as a business is important and can no longer be overlooked.

The excellent news is that where previous efforts might have fallen short, a renewed focus and current developments in this area - including in technology - give a factor for optimism that meaningful modification can be enacted.

This will need organizations to be actively anti-racist and commit to putting in the effort over the long term. It's an effort that's not likely to be squandered. Making development towards a more varied, equitable, and inclusive workplace ultimately benefits everyone - regardless of race.

FROM THE AUTHOR

Thank you for purchasing this book. I really enjoyed writing every part of it, and I hope to have great feedback from readers who enjoy the book. I hope you, too, enjoy it.

I appreciate that you chose to buy and read my book over some of the others out there. Thank you for putting your confidence in me to help you. If you enjoyed the book and have a couple of spare minutes now, it would really help me if you would like to leave me a review (even if it's short) on Amazon. All these reviews will help me spread the word about my books and encourage me to write more books!

Sincerely yours,

DR. MICHAEL W. COUCH

Made in the USA
Middletown, DE
14 June 2022

66800639R00062